The Bu
Our Brā

The Bug in Our Brain

How Raising Your Self-Worth Clears the Path to Success

Robert Christiansen

DEDICATION

To my beautiful wife, Kim. Thank you for all your support and belief in me.

CONTENTS

INTRODUCTION

Congratulations! You've made an incredible decision, one that could radically change the course of your life. I'm happy for you because I know what is ahead and how dramatic the changes in your life can be. Lao-Tzu would say, "You have taken the first step of a thousand mile journey."

I've written this book because I have a burning desire to change the world, one dream at a time. For a man who let others tell him what he should be and how he should do it, I've come to the realization that I've never defined what success looked like for me. I fell under the hypnotic effect of consumerism, résumés, and assets instead of listening to the pleading inner voice of my soul. More to the point, I never felt worthy of pursuing my definition of "success." It was easier to borrow yours and pretend I knew what I was doing.

The world's definition of "success" is constantly changing, and we're not sure as to where we should put our efforts. For decades we've been told to go to college, get a degree, secure a job with a great company, work, save, and hopefully retire to a beautiful sunset of a life well lived. Unfortunately, that's not how things are working out. A college degree does not equate to a great-paying job, the life expectancy of a Fortune 500 company is fifteen years, down from seventy-five, and retirement funds are not protected from runaway Enron behavior. The ground beneath our feet is constantly shifting. Technology is moving faster than ever, disrupting every industry, turning long-standing careers on their heads. The tried and true definition of "success" is gone, never to return in color or form. We are left without a rudder.

We need a new definition of "success," and it must come from within.

This book is about "self-worth," a term not commonly used and often misunderstood. "Self-worth" is, by definition, another term for "self-esteem." Yet, when we press

into the language of worthiness, we discover emotions that contribute to confidence but also sow the seed of self-sabotage. At its core, self-worth is the foundation of self-esteem, it is the root of confidence, it is the platform by which we decide our future, and it is the bat we use to beat ourselves. The purpose of this book is to elevate your self-worth and bring forth the desire and confidence to pursue your dreams.

The bug in your brain is self-worth, and through the exercises in this book, you have the opportunity to change how you see yourself.

From my perspective as a former computer programmer, we have bugs in our programming. These bugs feed our internal definition of "self-worth" and control every decision we make, whether we know it or not. By lifting self-worth, we patch the limiting bugs of beliefs and behaviors that hold us back from achieving success.

I'm not a licensed therapist, nor do I have a doctorate in psychology. I'm an entrepreneur, speaker, coach, and cloud-computing expert. I've coached men and women for twenty-five years and developed a program of common- and not-so-common-sense practices that change lives. In this book I share my experience and strength and hope that you too can elevate your worthiness to live the life of your dreams.

I've organized the text into three sections. In the first section, I explore self-worth and the strange behaviors we seem to be powerless to overcome. I introduce new terms and theories I've discovered over the course of my experience and present them in an easy-to-consume format.

In the second section, I dive into the vast array of bugs in our brain that stand in the way of success. Whether your goals are money, improved relationships, better physical health, making an impact on society, or finding spiritual enlightenment, the bugs of self-worth were programmed early in life. They are cemented in our routines until we replace them with language, images, and emotions that are aligned with what we want, that is, our definition of "success."

Finally, in the third section, I outline a program that lifts self-worth and changes how you go about achieving success. You will accomplish more in less time because you will no longer be fighting yourself. When you feel worthy of success, you naturally take actions that build a worthy and successful life. There's no more fighting the subconscious desires and distractions that tear down your goals. You'll smile and laugh more, be at peace with your progress, and feel like you are part of, instead of a piece of.

Thank you for the effort. I look forward to hearing about your success as we all come together in common purpose.

The world is a better place when we lift our worthiness.

Robert Christiansen

PART 1

THE POWER OF
SELF-WORTH

CHAPTER 1

WHY SELF-WORTH MATTERS

The Worthy Shall Prosper

The deeply personal and complex human traits of worthiness, deserving, self-value, and self-esteem, govern our success. How we value ourselves plays such a critical role in what opportunities we pursue that it can hardly be overstated. Self-worth is an ever-changing pair of glasses that broadens or limits our view of the world, colors every life experience, and propels us to take action or grounds us in stagnation. Self-worth is the foundation of all our choices, all our reactions, and all our efforts. It's the power that governs our abilities to overcome self-destructive behaviors. Self-worth is the key to our success and the saboteur of our plans.

The purpose of life is to create. However, most of us don't know what we want—which means we don't know what we want to create. Everyone wants money, but money without happiness is a living hell. Money is an amplifier of your emotional state and self-worth. Obtain money without the foundation of worthiness and it only magnifies our deeper character flaws.

There are those who pursue happiness but have no idea what real happiness means. Mankind has searched for happiness since the dawn of time and with little obvious success. What makes a person happy? Most will say peace and love, yet in what form, from what source, and for how long? There are many happy and content people, yet when asked to articulate what makes them joyful, they have a hard time delivering the message. It can be frustrating as hell to see what you want and be completely powerless to obtain it.

The fallback position to our power dilemma is to whitewash it in dissatisfaction and downplay our worthiness. We simply avoid discussing the topic of our true, God-given wishes because they're so out of reach.

If we don't know what we want, then how are we to recognize our dream life when it comes around? There are those who know what they what, but most will dismiss the opportunity as out of reach and rationalization it away. Why do we dismiss, play down, and outright deny our deepest desires? We're born with a voice deep within our soul, urging us to live our dream and become what we must become. Yet, for many, the hopeful voice is set on fire by criticism and fueled by regret.

Why do we deny the one thing that is most important to all humans?

Because we feel we don't deserve the gifts that come with living our dream life.

The media is full of examples. Sport figures attain the peak of their profession only to light a match and burn it down. Politicians, business professionals, husbands and wives, artists, and a million other examples of normal individuals attaining their dreams only to do something foolish to destroy it.

Yet, we can't deny our heart. You're reading this book because I've struck a cord and it's vibrating in your chest. It's the vibration of the possibility of your dream coming true. But you don't dare amplify the sound for fear of criticism, isolation, and self-sabotage.

If we're not worthy of receiving a gift, then we train ourselves to either ignore or dismiss it when it appears. For most of us, the training happened as a child, and now we live out our lives frustrated, wishing we had the ability to just make something happen, but instead we slip back into our old ways and beat ourselves up for not having the power to change.

This is the Bug in Our Brain—malformed self-worth. Worthiness controls our success and lights the match that burns it down. Self-worth is the fuel that moves us to action and turns our attention away just before we win the race.

There is a way out.

The purpose of this book is to lift your self-worth high enough so you feel deserving of the search for and eventually the finding of your passion.

The point of life is to live your life; it is to act out your life and to participate with others in the living of life. Laughter, love, passion, sorrow, pain, and joy are the flavors and colors of our world. When you believe you're worthy of love, then the pain and sorrow of a loss can be endured and transcended. You can truly experience a beautiful life when you believe you're worthy of receiving the gifts life has to offer.

However, it's hard to focus on attaining your dream life when you're unable to feed your child or get medical care. For many, daily living is a harsh reality. This book and the solutions within it fall on deaf ears when life is kicking your butt. Who can focus on health in the face of disease? How do we see wealth in the darkness of poverty?

Pain relief and distraction seem to be our only answers.

There is another way.

I'm here as a testament to the power of higher self-worth. Self-worth, backed by belief, will place you on the road to success.

When I was a young boy, all I wanted to do was play baseball. I was the kid who hung out at the park waiting for the other baseball-obsessed children, hoping to squeeze in a few innings before dinner. In the movie *The Sandlot*, Tom Guiry plays Scotty Smalls, a desperately self-conscious boy who gets in a lot of trouble when he takes his step-father's Babe Ruth autographed, one-of-a-kind, baseball to the sandlot. When the icon is lost to a ball-eating dog called The Beast, Smalls and his new friends set out to recover it before his step-father discovers it missing. *The Sandlot* is one of my top ten all-time favorite movies because I am Smalls. I so desperately wanted friends and would do anything to get them, including waiting for hours at the sandlot in a painful effort to be liked.

I do love baseball. My coaches were excellent and encouraged me through middle school and into high school. I even won a small college scholarship in my junior year because I had the highest batting average on the team and was a solid player. I was definitely not tracking for the major leagues but for sure NCAA opportunities.

Then something happened right after I won the scholarship. I shut down and lost interest. Our family moved to Washington, DC, the summer of my senior year, and I never played baseball again. I didn't even try out.

In hindsight, the dream of playing baseball in college got too close to becoming a reality. There are those who sprint to opportunities; however, I turned and walked away. That year, I got distracted with computers, and any dream of playing baseball was lost.

Looking back, I can see it clearly now: why I turned away from baseball and my dream of playing at higher levels. Operating from a basis of low self-worth, I avoided

taking the obvious action that would certainly move me a lot closer to my dream. The reality of a baseball college scholarship exceeded my capacity to accept it. I didn't feel worthy of receiving it.

A few months after I turned away from baseball, I started a downhill slide that lasted eight horrible years. The dam of self-loathing broke, and there was nothing I could do to stop the flood. I turned to alcohol and drugs in my early twenties to ease the amazing depths of my loneliness. On the surface, I wanted to play baseball, but what was really happening was much more serious. I needed something to take away the anxiety, and alcohol proved to be an effective and powerful solution.

Those years were brutal. I found computers in 1979 and discovered I had a high degree of talent. The obsessive nature of programming gave me a great place to hide. Computers do what you tell them—always. They never talk back unless you tell them to talk back. They have bugs in their programming because someone unintentionally or intentionally put the bug in the computer. For an alcoholic, it was the perfect tool to distract me from myself.

During that time I ignored the major bugs in my brain's programming and poured painkillers into my body. For a time, it worked. I could maneuver through life, faking it, until the day came when the painkillers stopped working. My programs demanded a reboot. I knew I'd die if I didn't make a serious and dramatic change.

On May 13, 1987, at the age of twenty-five, I got sober. However, the drinking and drug abuse were merely symptoms of much deeper and more troubling problems. The crushing reality of my self-worth didn't disappear when I stopped drinking. It took hard work and the guidance of mentors and friends to get me headed in the right direction.

Over the years I've come to realize that we all have bugs in our brains. It's the bug of deformed self-worth. It lives in our subconscious, influencing our decisions and controlling our actions. At times, we seem to be at war with our higher self. We consciously want to be successful, but lack the power to make the changes necessary to achieve our goals.

I know that I'm an extreme case. I've replaced the more serious bugs with new beliefs, images, and values. I still wrestle with the remaining defects of character, yet on the whole, I love my life and all those I share it with.

Now, thirty years later, with thousands of encounters as a student and a mentor to those who want a better life, I know my greatest joy comes from witnessing the success of others. I seek a greater love and all that comes with it. I feel worthy of saying "Yes!" to all that life has to offer. My hope and belief is that you'll find what I have found. You definitely don't need to be an alcoholic to benefit from the tools in this book. What I know is this: the tools work for all those who use them—people of any shape, size, color, and creed. From Yale to jail, from Park Place to park bench, we all can benefit from higher self-worth.

Build your self-worth. Learn where the language of negative self-worth originates, and replace it with deserving. This book shows you how and what to expect when success suddenly and rapidly comes your way. Success does create problems. You'll need someone who understands what to do when you exceed your self-worth limit. I've been there, and I can tell you that exceeding your self-worth limit is very tricky. That's why I've written this book and established a coaching practice with a specific focus on lifting our clients' self-worth and overcoming their self-worth barriers.

From time to time, I'll speak of God in this book. I am a spiritual man and with no particular religious practice. I've taken what I've needed from the world's religions and left the rest. What I believe is this: there is a power that listens to me 24-7, and it responds positively to my desires. Therefore, I must use caution as to the words and emotions I carry in my mind.

The solutions in this book change the language, images, and emotions of your thinking so you can tell God what you want. Self-worth is the root of all desire, and by lifting your worthiness, you elevate the quality of your life.

You can experience success as you define success. If tens of thousands of men and women who suffered from the extreme depths of loathing can lift their self-worth and live amazing lives, so can you.

Take the actions outlined in this book. I've arranged it to be an easy and consumable read with stories, personal examples, and testimonies from those who've lifted their worthiness and found great happiness in the pursuit of their dreams.

I hope to see you soon and to connect along the way.

CHAPTER 2

ALMOST SOMEBODY

Worthiness moves you past the fear of making a mistake.

In early 1998, I completed my second novel called *Trojan Horse*. A thriller set in Irvine, California, the fast-paced, hi-tech drama pitted moral and social common sense against the wild times of the dot-com era and the rampant collective hysteria that seemed to overwhelm even the most conservative investors. I'd received several positive responses from literary agents, a rarity for an unknown author, and was excited about the prospects of getting my work into the mainstream.

I selected a well-known agent, and we spoke about the book over the phone. She liked it a lot and thought it had potential. However, she wanted me to change how the main character became aware of the growing danger around him.

"What's dramatic about dropping a lobster in a pot and turning up the heat?" she asked, not waiting for my response. "Nothing."

"Now, hang a lobster over a boiling pot of water and threaten to drop him in," she continued. "Now that's dramatic."

She was right. My main character needed a dramatic boost and I knew exactly how to do it.

The changes were easy to make and definitely an improvement. The plot line of the characters would support the new flow, and we agreed to talk when the changes were made. In the meantime, she would float the first chapter by her friends at Warner Bros. and see what was what.

Wow! This was better than I could imagine. All I had to do was rewrite a few chapters and we were on our way to the next level. It wasn't a book deal, but from everything I had learned about the industry, this was definitely significant. My writing teacher was really excited and confirmed the rarity of gaining attention so quickly.

I made the first changes within a week and was on a clear path to finalizing the next revision of *Trojan Horse*.

Then the wheels fell off. My clarity of purpose slipped away like a fox in the night. I found myself questioning the rewrites and constantly criticizing the work. *What if she doesn't like the changes?* was the common narrative each time I sat down at the keyboard. The nagging fear of rejection haunted me as I tried to make the simplest of changes. The confidence of the week prior was lost in the wake of self-doubt, and I dropped into the world of uncertainty. I no longer trusted my abilities.

Weeks turned into months. Predictably, the literary agent lost interest; she wasn't going to track me down and force me to do my work. That's the author's burden, and she knew it very well. My wife encouraged me to keep going but was equally at a loss as to why I suddenly retracted from success as if it were a hot flame.

Trojan Horse never saw the final revisions. I put the work on pause and walked away.

For years, *Trojan Horse* stood as the monumental failure of my inability to conquer fear. Success was on the other side of the river. I could see it clearly, yet the fear of actually achieving success with *Trojan Horse* prevented me from swimming to the other side.

For the next fifteen years, I tried to untangle the ropes that held me back. Not being satisfied with a whitewashing of psychobabble, I wanted to know if there was a root cause to my issue and if there were any practical steps I could take to overcome the problem. From what I could see among my peers, colleagues, and friends, the problem touched everybody, yet there appeared to be few solutions that dealt with the core issue and even fewer that had developed a program to address it.

What I found is the basis of this book. There is a Bug in Our Brain that prevents us from success beyond what we were programmed to accept, or if you would, what we believe we're worthy of receiving. If our success exceeds our programmed worthiness level, the bug activates sabotage behaviors that destroy our winnings and move us back to our preprogrammed worthiness state.

Trojan Horse pushed me well beyond my ability to handle success. I simply didn't feel worthy of the attention the book was receiving; my programming didn't allow it. My subconscious mind, programmed at an early age, said *This is more than you deserve*, and the rest was history. My inner dialog chastised and punished me for daring to believe in my dreams. The voice of self-worth told me, *I'm not good enough to write this book. No one will read it, so why even try?*

For years I tried programs, books, healings, churches, seminars, events, and the Internet to instill in me the power to change. I remember speaking with a good friend who suggested that I turn within and follow a well-known yogi. I'm certain the path to enlightenment is well paved…for those who believe they deserve to walk it.

Even more challenging was the voice I didn't hear. It was the compulsive and habitual cry of my subconscious keeping me from any experience that remotely looked different from what it believed I was worthy of receiving. You see, from an early age, I'd been programmed for a predefined level of success—as determined by those who may or may not have had my best interests in mind.

Don't get me wrong. I've lived an amazing life. I got sober when I was twenty-five and have not had a drink or drug for thirty years. I've made a good living as a computer scientist, executive, and entrepreneur. I am a great husband, father, mentor, and friend.

That said, I never truly felt happy with my success. It lacked meaning and purpose. I felt like a hamster on a wheel, running in place because that's what everyone else was doing. In the early days of my sobriety, I was deeply grateful to come out of a drunken stupor and live a normal life. Yet, once I had attained what I believed was success, the hollowness of the hamster wheel tore at me until I could no longer ignore it.

For thirty years I've worked with alcoholic men and women who suffer from mind-boggling self-worth issues. Few know the depths of self-loathing the addicted face every day. I'm not a trained psychologist or a licensed therapist. I am a cloud-computing expert by day and a mentor, speaker, and coach by night. The basis of my conclusions is rooted in the practical application of real-world, knee-to-knee, eye-to-eye techniques and exercises that anyone can implement in their life. You do not have to be a drug addict to benefit from this discovery.

What I *do* offer is a path to success as defined by you. Success is different for everyone, and for most of us, the level of success was set when we were young and didn't have a choice in the matter. You're in a battle with your subconscious programming, and it's a thousand times stronger than you know.

The purpose of this book is to help you understand the nature of worthiness and how it affects every aspect of your world. Literally, your success in life is directly linked to the level you believe you deserve.

You are holding in your hands the master key to unlocking your success. By re-programming your brain, you're able to achieve your deepest desires in a surprisingly short amount of time.

There are bugs in your programming, and yes, you can update the app!

CHAPTER 3

HOW WE SEE OURSELVES

The flawed and healed rescue the wounded.

Looking back, I never truly understood the battle. I was frustrated with my inability to change and control my self-sabotaging behavior. When I speak of self-sabotaging behavior, I mean the actions I wish I had the power to stop. I call them character defects; others call them the deadly sins. In the end, they're behaviors that are not good for me. A partial list includes overeating, gambling, credit-card debt, arguing, procrastination, selfishness, isolating, and a host of other vices I wish I could put down.

For example, body image is a serious problem for both women and men. I don't look like the male models in *Men's Health* magazine. They obviously have more money, flatter abs, stronger muscles, and are packing more heat than I. There was a time when I looked at myself in the mirror and saw an ugly man. When I looked down, all I could see was my stomach. Not good for any man's self-esteem.

It's hard to love yourself with the "you look like shit" negative self-worth voice in my head. I didn't realize how negative that voice had become until one day, while dissecting my body in the mirror, I put my hands on my stomach, squeezed the fat roll and looked into my eyes and said, "How can I attract success if I don't even value myself physically?"

I can't overstate the importance of this fact—self-worth, self-esteem, and self-love are the foundation of a successful life. They're the basis by which we build our dreams and get what we want. I must change the narrative in my mind including the language, images, and emotions that support the well-being of my complete life, including my body. It's the temple in which I live. I'm not separate from my body but one with it. Therefore, I must see it as a gift.

The purpose of this book is to build your self-worth in all areas of your life. Nothing is more important to you right now. Everything hinges upon it.

CHAPTER 4

MY EXPERIENCE

Lost to the blind is the beauty of the morning sky.

I'm a father of three, married for twenty-five years, and a great role model for my family, friends, and community. I've a deep worthiness related to my abilities as a father and a husband. However, if asked about my abilities to attain my goals, I'd respond differently.

During these years, I had a mentor named Tony Fisher. Tony was a great man and taught me a lot about self-worth. Prior to his passing, Tony asked me two simple questions that helped me understand what was happening inside of me. They are:

1. *What is God to me?*
2. *What am I to God?*

The first question was easy. God got me sober and provided me a great sober life. He intervened when I had nowhere to go. Without God's help, I'd be dead. This is my truth. I know what God is to me.

The second question was much, much harder. I had no idea what I was to God. To be honest, I didn't think God much cared for me. The will of God seemed random and didn't fit my values. Moreover, my deeper, more glaring character defects had yet to be removed. I'm referring to procrastination, envy, sloth, greed, and the like. I prayed to have better control over my anger, but the defect persisted. I prayed to learn how to advance in my career, but sloth and resentment would creep in and stop my progress. My thinking got pretty ugly. From my perspective, God didn't know who I was, nor did he care much about me.

When I dug deeper, I found a hot set of childhood memories that condemned God for not protecting me when I was little. If I was something to God, then where was God when I was a kid? I needed protection, and he was nowhere to be found!

Deep down, I cursed God. It's why I dropped out of the Catholic Church at sixteen years old, cast dispersions on the holy rollers, sneered at those with deep convictions, mocked devotees in robes, and laughed at the masses for being cattle.

When all the shouting and psychobabble was done, I believed God abandoned me. With that nasty bug in my programming, how could I live with the knowledge that God got me sober and gave me a great life?

I couldn't! It doesn't fit in my logic. Yet, when dealing with subconscious programming that is founded in childhood injury, logic leaves the building. The bug in my programming is not logical; it causes crazy behaviors and it's unpredictable. It's a flaw in execution.

Do I deserve God's love?

No! Not when I was a kid, and not now because he doesn't seem to be listening.

Dysfunctional thinking lurked below the surface of my consciousness. On one side I had the grateful mind of a rescued alcoholic. On the other side, I lived with the schizophrenic identity of an abused child. Why would God save me from an alcoholic death only to torture me with character defects that never seemed to change? God's plan didn't make sense.

Wasn't I a great father and wonderful husband? Yes, but why am I so unhappy and unfulfilled?

On the surface, I had everything nailed down: a great family, a wonderful partner, a good income, a couple of cars, nice living arrangements—the works. However, as soon as I reached a certain level of success, I'd light a match and set the building on fire. Occasionally, I would catch myself before the flames got too high, but most of the times, I would self-rationalize and justify my behavior by blaming others for what they were doing to me.

I asked God to remove my character defects of spending and credit-card debt. They didn't go. Frustrated, I'd ask a different way, pray longer, go on fasts, change my eating habits, listen to speakers, attend seminars, sleep more, and meditate—on and on. For twenty years! I tried every known possible way to break through my success barrier.

There had to be another way!

Maybe I'm undisciplined?

Here's the problem: I have disciplines out the ass. I know I'm a disciplined man. Hell, I've been sober for three decades, since I was twenty-five years old. You don't stay sober for that long without a complete understanding of human nature and the requirement of discipline to manage your life.

But there it was—my lack of discipline and unmanageability. How could I have disciplines in so many areas of my life, yet, not have them around the key areas of success? What was the problem? How were other men and women able to achieve success and I was not?

Let me tell you, this drove me mad. The older I got, the more my frustration grew. With each passing year, and then decade, I saw others passing me by while the cliff of retirement rapidly approached. All I could see was my wife and I becoming more and more of a burden on our children as I fell into a pit of self-pity and failure.

I stopped blaming others for my problems long ago. You can't achieve long-term sobriety while blaming others for your life. You learn to take responsibility for all your actions. Therefore, I'm a failure—100 percent ownership—a failure.

The Gut Punch

I co-founded a cloud computing company serving small to medium size businesses. Like all start-ups, we struggled to get the business off the ground, and the first year was a constant series of failures and lessons learned. After several months, we figured out the sales model and established a small but growing base of business. However, it wasn't enough for our primary investor, and they defunded the venture. I didn't blame them. They wanted to see greater success in a shorter time frame than we were able to produce.

With the brick wall of failure approaching quickly, I shuffled expenses, landed more business, and was able to get the endeavor to break even. It was a big win. The business model was looking better, and we felt we were on the right track. The light at the end of the tunnel appeared to be something other than an oncoming train.

Then the wheels came off. We lost our largest client, and in two months, more than half our revenue would disappear. Without new clients, we would certainly close the doors. Through heroic efforts, we landed just enough new business to cover expenses, pay myself a minimal wage, and keep the support staff in place. We bare-ly kept the lights on. I borrowed money to cover my living expenses for a couple of months, but it wasn't looking good.

It all came to a head when my wife said, "I'm so worried about money that my hair is falling out."

What a gut punch! I looked at her pleading eyes and felt completely helpless. One more time, I tried to build my dream and one more time I missed. How could I change when I didn't even understand the problem?

When my wife lost faith in me, I felt like a wounded animal. Sooner or later, the wolves would arrive and scavenge what was left.

For a time, I was lost in self-pity and believed I was beyond help. Like those drug addicts who've cooked their brain beyond repair, I too appeared to be without hope. You know you're screwed when you thank God for your sober life and, at the same time, tell Him to kiss your ass for the results.

Something Had to Change

Over the years, numerous well-meaning friends suggested meditation. I tried to quiet my mind only to pour more gasoline on the raging fire of my worthiness. With each failed attempt to calm my thinking, I added another narrative to the long list of nega-tive self-talk that filled my head.

I joined a group in Laguna Beach, California that practiced group meditation every Thursday morning. A different member of the group would lead the twenty-minute session in an effort to expose us to new practices and routines. During one of the sessions, a childhood memory flashed in my mind's eye. I tried to put it down, but the pain of the experience rose and grabbed me by the throat.

When I was ten, I'd play truth or dare with the neighborhood kids. One of the other boys was a skinny kid we'll call Joey for now. Instead of telling the truth, Joey opted for the dare. The other kids and I took turns spitting on his face. It was not my finest moment and one that I truly regret. Joey's father discovered us in the backyard, torturing his son, and put an end to the madness.

The shame of this memory wouldn't leave me. Whenever I closed my eyes to meditate, all I could see was Joey enduring the torture for the sake of being wanted

and fitting in with our group. Every time I tried to calm my mind, the disgusting event and all its shame flashed in my head, and I'd see Joey's face covered in spit. My logical, rational thinking would kick in and say, *You were ten, doing stupid kid things. Get over it and move on!*

What I know now is that hurt people inflict harm on others. Even at the age of ten, I was a hurt child, wanting to hurt other children. Deep down, I felt tremendous guilt. Guilt is the anchor of stunted self-worth.

I knew something had to change.

I wrote two letters—one to Joey (who was now forty-five) and one to his father (who was still friends with my Dad). In both letters I took responsibility for my behavior and the harm it caused Joey and his family. I asked if there was anything I could do to make it right. I sent both letters to Joey's father and asked him to forward the other letter to his son if he felt it was appropriate.

Two weeks after I mailed the letters, Joey's father called me. He explained that we were good kids and would've been proud to have us as his own. That wasn't the response I was expecting. I thanked him for the compliment. He told me he forwarded the other letter to his son.

A week later I received a call. Joey said he didn't remember the incident but was happy to hear from me. He didn't hold any grudge against our family or me, and wished us well. I remember exactly where I was when we hung up. It was 3:00 p.m. on a sunny spring day in Aliso Viejo, California. I felt a great freedom and was grateful that I followed my intuition and made the amends.

A few months later, Joey died of a heart attack at forty-five. The news stunned me. To this day I'm perplexed as to the sequence of these events, but I am grateful that I listened to my inner voice. I had slayed one of many dragons, and I was released from its power. I patched the bug in my programming.

Up to that point, I had rationalized away my behavior and more importantly my self-worth with "adult language" that released me from the obligation of owning my life. It was somebody else's fault and not mine.

Here are a few statements I used to keep myself unworthy:

"You were too young to know better."
"It was not your fault."
"You cannot be expected to understand when you were so young."

"The past is the past; there is nothing you can do about it."
"You already made peace with what happened. Why are you rehashing it?"
"Why do you keep pulling up the past?"

I felt like I had a broken leg that never healed quite right. In the beginning, I dealt with the pain through drinking and drug abuse. Then, when the effects of drugs and alcohol no longer worked, I cleared the obvious wreckage and built a good life. I did what I believed a "normal person" should do. However, the bug in my programming still remained and prevented me from achieving any success that was more than I deserved.

Lurking well below the surface of my subconscious were voices that rattled around like marbles in a dryer. I realized that I needed to deal with them like never before. No longer was it OK to ignore or rationalize away the bugs of my childhood. I had to summon the courage to face them.

At an early age, I was imprinted with images and experiences that formed the foundation of my self-worth. What I know is that a child needs safety and validation. Without safety, a child develops a core self-image grounded in fear and anxiety. Without valuation, a child's self-worth becomes the limiting factor in their adult life.

Having had three children of my own, two that were parented with safety and validation, and one that was not, I have firsthand experience as to the validity of my opinion. I've worked with hundreds of men and women who are the by-product of a childhood without safety and validation. The common theme among all of them is low self-worth.

How I valued myself is directly related to the events that occurred when I was young. It wasn't my fault; I was dealt a bad hand. I didn't get what I needed from my parents. As well my parents were unable to give me something they didn't have—also not their fault.

However, it is my responsibility.

My case was quite severe. Although the surface of the water appeared calm, violent currents drove every single choice I made. My demons needed to come up and out, and without help, I was destined to repeat the same behavior expecting a different result. For the first time, the glass ceiling was in view, and I could see the problem for what it was.

Through my healing process came the recognition that higher self-worth is the key to my success. I discovered that the bug in my childhood programming prevented me from moving forward. I lacked the programs that others seem to execute.

If I could patch the most difficult bugs, I wondered if I could install new programming that would help me achieve success?

As it turned out, the answer is *yes*!

Finding the Bugs

I turned the mirror on myself and started on a rigorous course of action. I read every spiritual and self-help book I could find on changing subconscious thought. I consumed three or four books a month. I practiced exercises and routines that promised to change my thinking. Most were useless because they didn't deal with the underlying issue of self-worth.

However, there are good authors, teachers and coaches who understand the power of routine and the impact it has on our brain. There were a few methods for changing subconscious thought that worked for me. Here are the techniques that helped me isolate and correct the bugs in my worthiness.

- Dramatic spiritual or emotional events
- Affirmations and repetition
- Meditation
- Emotional freedom techniques (EFT) tapping, which is a form of energy therapy

In my experience, strong spiritual and emotional change is hard to reproduce. Moments of clarity are rare. We can't count on them as a reliable technique to change our thinking as they are too hard to reproduce. I've had three or four significant events that changed how I saw myself, but they were not planned or created. I needed tools within my control to find the bugs, and a spiritual experience doesn't offer the consistency.

What worked for me were affirmations, meditation, EFT tapping, and a coach who knew how to lead people through success. I discovered I have more problems with success than I do failure. From my perspective, human beings know how to carry on when faced with real challenges but lack skill in handling success.

In his groundbreaking book *The Road Less Traveled*, Dr. M. Scott Peck wonderfully describes the fundamental problem with most mental illness. Dr. Peck reasons that children deprived of validation grow up with core self-worth issues that result in all sorts of character defects. They also exhibit self-destructive behaviors ranging from overeating to alcoholism to drug addiction.

I learned about neuroplasticity, which is the brain's ability to reorganize itself by forming new neural connections. There is overwhelming evidence that meditation and prayer changes the shape and effectiveness of your brain. I decided to put this theory to the test. I wrote mantras, prayers, and affirmations, and read them out loud every morning.

My self-worth changed immediately.

The status quo of my failing cloud company was no longer acceptable. My new language of higher self-worth would not allow the current situation. People who elevate self-worth take action to fix problems. I didn't like the way the company was going and decided to do something about it. I was the technology brains behind the company but lacked the confidence to leverage it. Without me, the engine would stop. It was time for a change.

Within a week, I negotiated the buyout of two partners and owned the controlling majority of shares. I knew we didn't have a fundable business venture in the classic sense. It was a good little company but lacked cash reserves. I decided to sell it and move on.

As I practiced my affirmations and meditation every day, I found I could change the programming of my self-worth by changing the language of my thinking. Instead of operating from a basis of fear and doubt, I insisted on positive language at every step of the sale of the business. I believed I could sell the company for a good price and that belief carried me forward with confidence and motivation. Within a month, I found a good buyer for the company, executed the transaction, and transitioned the company to the new owners. More importantly, I settled all the outstanding company debt in full and cleared all my personal debt, which was welcome news and relief to my wife.

I couldn't have asked for a better outcome.

The Solution

During the sale of my cloud company, a good friend and I formed a mastermind group with other like-minded professionals who were focused on wealth attainment. We formulized my exercises and readings, and structured disciplines based on the science of routine. It didn't take long to see results with the sales of my company the primary example. People wanted to know what we were doing and if they could go through it as well. Feeling a deep desire to share what we'd learned, we introduced a four-week course based on the book *The Science of Getting Rich* by Wallace Wattles. Wattles's book was groundbreaking for me, and I spent many an hour pulling together what I believed was working in my life.

Repetition is the foundation of change, and I'd used affirmations to align my thinking with my goals. And not just any affirmations, I wrote my own, specific to exactly what I wanted.

And that brings us to a very important point: knowing what you want. What I wanted was to feel better about myself. I wanted to eliminate the negative self-talk and replace it with positive language and emotion that supported my goals.

I continued to refine and consolidate the exercises and measure the results. Every six months, each member of the mastermind group presented their progress. The presentations required full transparency. We detailed our balance sheet down to every credit card, account, and asset. We discussed health, relationships, kids, and spiritual progress. Nothing was off limits.

The results were undeniable. I dramatically improved every category of my life. I successfully changed the underlying self-worth settings and removed the glaring bugs from my brain.

The Success Statement

The success statement is a document of your wants and dreams, written with gratitude and in present tense. While selling my company, I listed the goals I wanted to achieve, clearly detailing the revenue, reputation, and opportunities I believe were necessary to achieve my goal. I read my success statement every day, telling no one except my wife and a group of close friends. When I achieve one of the goals, I changed the statement to include another higher goal, and so on. I treated the document like a loose garment, allowing it to move with me, unrestricted. With each success accomplished, with each goal attained, my worthiness was lifted. Confidence and motivation are fed by self-worth. Be specific with what you want, train your subconscious mind to accept it as routine thinking, and stay close to a coach who understands how to keep you focused as you hit each plateau of success.

When positive thinking becomes your subconscious routine, it becomes instinct. You no longer struggle with self-doubt, character defects, and negative self-talk. You naturally and effortlessly eat the right foods, attract new and better opportunities, smile more, love more, and gain confidence where there was none. You see your fellows as cocreators and try to help them whenever and wherever possible. It is a natural process that takes less and less effort with each expansion of higher self-worth.

Read this book multiple times. The chapters are short and intended to drive a single point or lesson. I've added numerous testimonies of those who have lifted their self-worth and are living the life of their dreams. I've also added personal stories I hope you find as impactful as I have.

Higher self-worth is a gift. Lifting your self-worth puts you on the road to discovery and opens the doors to opportunities you never imagined possible. Knowing what you want is not enough. You must be worthy to receive it.

CHAPTER 5

AN EXTREME CASE

I found the key that unlocked the basement of my denial.

To some degree, every human being exhibits the same self-worth characteristics that are so obviously displayed in the practicing alcoholic.

For example, most of us know what to do to lose weight; we simply lack the power to take the right actions. This is no different than the practicing drug addict. We know what to do but lack the power to do it. We all are addicted—more or less—to some form of self-abuse. The consequences of our addictions depend upon the severity of our self-worth and the bugs in our programming. For some, self-worth mandates a harsh punishment of obesity, while others endure the lesser consequences of an additional fifteen pounds. Most people have resigned to their powerlessness and accepted their weight gain as fate.

Deep within the alcoholic is a sincere desire to stop. When honestly pressed against the wall, they all want to stop their destructive behavior. Then, when faced with the real possibility of death, alcoholics cry out for help and usually get it. They find their way into a detox or an AA group, sober up, and feel good—for a short period of time.

However, most don't stay sober.

I've witnessed thousands and thousands of alcoholics and addicts roll in and out of recovery without a clue to what ails them. We (those who have recovered) attribute their relapse to alcoholism—a chronic affliction of the mind and body that appears to have few treatments other than spiritual.

Over the years, I've noticed a common thread: the lack of self-worth. If alcoholics don't address their self-worth problem, they quickly decide that sobriety is not for them and leave. This behavior baffled me. Why would someone leave when there is overwhelming evidence of a treatment that works? Millions of people have recovered from drug and alcohol abuse. Yet, the newly sober, more often than not, turn away and leave. The only reason, at least from my position and daily exposure to this tragic cycle, is that alcoholics don't believe they deserve the good life sobriety has to offer.

Without significant reprogramming of their belief system, they return to their punishing behaviors. It is the primary reason they don't stay sober. Until there is a serious change in how they see themselves, nothing can be done.

This comparison of a chronic alcoholic and your particular powerlessness is not an exaggeration. Those who struggle with attaining their dream life grapple with the same self-worth issues that plague the alcoholic; it is just a matter of degree.

I struggled with weight most of my life, knowing full well what it took to achieve my goals. However, I lacked the power to change my behavior much like the alcoholic struggles to stop drinking. I'd rationalize eating fast food or skipping an exercise program, telling myself I could make up for it another day. In reality I didn't have the power to change because my bug of self-worth was too powerful.

The good news is self-worth can be lifted no matter the severity of your problem. You don't have to be an alcoholic or drug addict to lift your self-worth to remove the obstacles of success. Using the simple tools outlined in this book, you can eliminate the bug in your brain that prevents you from accepting success.

And yes, you're preventing your success.

CHAPTER 6

THE ROUTINE ENGINE

Worthiness is the foundation of confidence.

The human brain is amazing. Scientists and researchers are trying to understand how the brain works, yet they're constantly updating and changing their position. We know the basics of imprinting (how we learn) and retrieval (how we recall), but that seems to be constantly up for debate. The truth is we know so little about how the brain actually works. No two brains are alike; each one operates differently than another. Researchers try to make definite statements of fact, only to have additional research contradict it.

Our brain handles much more than we comprehend. Recent discoveries have determined that we develop 85 percent of our brain's neuron cells by the age of two. Unlike all the other cells in your body, which are replaced at regular intervals, the bulk of your neuron cells stay with you from birth and return to the earth at death. It's as if you're given a computer at birth with a set of primary programs and the ability to download new instructions.

Within the center of your brain is an oval cluster of neuron cells called the basil ganglia. In his wonderful book, *The Power of Habit: Why We Do What We Do in Life and Business*, Charles Duhigg details the groundbreaking research performed in the 1990s by the Brain and Cognitive Science department at MIT. They discovered that routines are learned, stored, and, in part, performed by the basil ganglia. More recent research points to other cooperative segments of the brain that assist in language, emotions, physical dexterity, and a host of other functions we often take for granted.

I call these collective brain functions the Routine Engine. Much like the operating system of a computer, the Routine Engine performs hundreds of programs on your behalf. Many are critical for your survival, for without them you'd die within a few minutes. Can you imagine having to focus on every breath to ensure your survival? The Routine Engine handles breathing and hundreds of other tasks for you so you can focus on high function activities.

The Routine Engine also has the capability to learn, store, and perform language and image routines. For example, consider a song that gets stuck in your head. We seem powerless to stop the run away thinking and repetitive force of the music. It's as if the Routine Engine is stuck in an infinite loop, and unless we're able to interrupt it, the song is habitually repeated.

Through habit, we can program the Routine Engine and replace limiting bugs with new, more up-to-date software that is aligned with our goals.

You didn't choose your first set of programs. You didn't even get to pick your own name, let alone have the choice of what is good, bad, moral, right, wrong, safe, or dangerous. For the most part, much of the programming we received as children was necessary. However, we inherited programming that does not serve us now; it stands in the way of our progress and the attainment of our dreams.

As a recovered alcoholic, I know the power of the Routine Engine and how difficult it can be to overcome bad programming. At the core of every alcoholic is extreme low self-worth coupled with the physical allergy of addiction. The alcoholic and drug addict must elevate their self-worth else they return to the cycle of abuse that, once started, is difficult to stop.

The process of changing self-worth in a newly recovered alcoholic is exceptionally hard. Their identity, enforced by the Routine Engine, is habitual and requires significant and purposeful changes in daily routines to lift self-worth. If self-worth is not lifted in the newly sober person, they struggle with accepting a better life. This is why alcoholics go back to drinking. They know they have a physical allergy that, once started, is hard to stop, yet go back to it anyway. It's crazy to think that a newly sober person would turn away from all the good that comes from a sober life, but that is exactly what they do. They say, "Thank you for all that you've done. I appreciate the offer, but I'm going back to abusing myself."

The Routine Engine and the programming of inferior self-worth are extreme in these cases. The reprogramming often requires a ninety-day detox with a lot of support.

Hopefully, you're not facing such extremes. Worthiness can be lifted and by lifting it, we change how we see the world.

If you're not satisfied with what you are getting out of life, then know there is a way to fix the bug in your brain. Your Routine Engine can be updated. By changing your programming, you change the limiting language and beliefs of self-worth. By changing the language in the Routine Engine to higher self-worth, we naturally direct our thinking to focus on success and the action to attain it.

Our new behavior becomes instinct. This is how we fix our bugs.

CHAPTER 7

THE SELF-WORTH THERMOSTAT

Stand on the legs of self-worth.

veryone has a self-worth thermostat. Much like the device in a home, your thermostat maintains the comfort zone of your worthiness. If you fall below your lower limit or break through the upper barrier, your brain triggers an emotional response meant to pull you back within your worthiness range. Our Routine Engine controls our self-worth temperature, and unless you adjust the settings, the programming will keep you locked between your upper and lower limits. This is the root of the problem—self-worth must be lifted to change the upper limit of your worthiness.

Imagine you share an office building with thirty coworkers. Your desk is near a window and gets hot from the midday sun. Each afternoon, you wander over to the thermostat and lower the temperature to sixty-eight degrees. You return to your desk happy and relax, knowing you've made a change for the better. Thirty minutes later, you're sweating and head back to the thermostat. You discover the temperature is still the same seventy-eight degrees it was the first time you tried to change it. Frustrated, you spin the dial left and right, to no avail.

You hear a voice. "The thermostat is disabled."

You turn and see a woman, ambivalence painted across her face. "What do you mean?" you reply.

Your friend points to the wall and says, "The device is fake, meant to give you the illusion that you're changing the temperature. It's the placebo effect."

You realize that there is something else controlling the temperature, and it's not you. You want to be cooler; however, another system is overriding your instructions and you're helpless to change it. The Routine Engine of your subconscious is the wizard behind the curtain. It's a thousand times more powerful than your consciousness.

The self-worth thermostat was set in your early days. Parents, family, friends, teachers, coaches, neighbors, bullies, and many others all contributed to your lower and upper self-worth limits. The Routine Engine of your mind maintains the self-worth settings so you can stay in your comfort zone. When you trip the thermostat of your comfort zone, fear and anxiety kicks in and tells you "This is not safe!" The Routine Engine engages old behaviors (overeating, spending, procrastination, anxiety, free-floating fear) and reinforces behaviors that move you back within the upper and lower limits.

It's a cycle the eats away at our confidence.

By the time clients make it to me, they're beaten and defeated, without a clue as to what has happened.

My Experience

The following events, images, and emotions formed the foundation of my worthiness. They were the bugs in my brain, securely lodged in my Routine Engine.

- A pack of school Bullies regularly knock my school books out of my hands
- A kid kicking me
- My dad telling me to shut up
- My mother and father fighting over money
- My dad calling my mother a shit bird
- My mother calling my father a dumb shit
- The family dog attacking me
- My parents withholding their approval
- A kid punching me

The language, emotions, and images of these scenes filled my subconscious and formed the foundation of my self-worth. I know my situation was severe. My Routine Engine's sole purpose is to keep me alive and safe—as defined by my environment. As a child, I assume I was at fault—for all of it—whatever "it" was.

The programming I received as a child was not my fault; I was dealt a bad hand. So it was for my mom and dad, their parents, and so on. However, it is my responsibility to play my cards as best I can. The insanity of ancestors could stop with me, if I made the decision and acted on it. I could choose to raise children with higher self-worth and stop handing down the same old programming my parents received at no fault of their own.

And that is exactly what I decided to do. I wanted new programs. I wanted new language and images that made me feel better about who I am and what I can do.

Below are my new, higher self-worth programs I used to replace the events and emotions of the list above. I gave my Routine Engine new stories to replace the old stories.

- My friends invite me to play baseball after school.
- My dad picks me up after school and gives me a big hug.
- My mom holds me after I trip and fall.
- My dad often says "Robert, I am proud of you."
- My grandma reads my favorite *Cat in the Hat* book when she babysits.
- My grandpa plays tag with me in the park.
- My dad lifts me up to pick an avocado off my grandparent's tree.
- My teacher sits with me and helps me understand a problem.
- I hit a double in baseball and see my parents cheering in the stands.
- My mom and dad often say "I love you."

I changed the temperature settings of my self-worth thermostat by giving my subconscious new language, images, and emotions. My Routine Engine is habitual and compulsive; I can upload new routines and naturally change the way I go about my life. Once the new programs are habitual, I instinctually do more right behavior with less energy. It's a beautiful way of life.

What events, emotions, and images do you want running your life? You can choose the old painful ones or the new, more beautiful thoughts and beliefs that support what you want. This process requires courage to face the deeper and darker wounds of your youth. It's worth the investment.

CHAPTER 8

THE VEHICLE OF YOUR SUCCESS

All doors need to be opened.

When your Routine Engine is aligned with your desires, you naturally focus on the actions that accelerate your attainment. Worthy people work less and achieve more because they're not fighting their Routine Engine; they let the habitual and compulsive thought system make great decisions on their behalf. As a result, they get more done, achieve more, and are less stressed and seem to be happy most of the time.

Consider the analogy of a bicycle as your vehicle of success.

Riding a bicycle is a complicated affair; however, for most of us, it is a skill we learned as children and retain to this day.

When I taught our kids how to ride a bike, new fears surfaced I'd never seen in them before. On one hand, they were terrified of bodily harm, and on the other hand, they deeply desired to master the skill. Their desire to ride a bike exceeded their paralyzing fear.

Our daughter, Emily, never to be outdone, rode her bicycle before her older brother. She cried and screamed at me, all the while begging me to show her how to ride the two-wheeled monster. Once she mastered it, she took off and, to this day, has never looked back. Our son, Taylor, in his own way, saw his sister accomplish the goal and within minutes of her success was up and riding. As a father, I beamed with delight as my children mastered their fears and glowed in the light of success.

Our vehicle of success is much like mastering a bicycle.

Confidence
Motivation
Action

Worthiness
Options
Choice

The front wheel is *worthiness*.

We steer toward what we believe we deserve. The higher our self-worth, the more destinations we see. We exercise the power of choice by choosing our goals. Every goal we desire must first appear achievable; otherwise we ignore it as an option. We steer toward goals we feel we are worthy of accomplishing.

The back wheel is *confidence*.

Confidence is the power and the speed at which we ride after our goals. The more confidence we have, the faster we pedal toward the goals. Pedaling is the action we take that moves us closer to success.

When we combine worthiness (steering) and confidence (power), we pedal to what we want. Apply more confidence and we pedal faster. Increase our worthiness; increase the number of opportunities we see as goals.

You decide where you want to ride and how fast you want to pedal. If you want to get to your goals faster, then lift your self-worth higher. This will expand your vision and increase your confidence. You'll spend less energy riding toward destinations that are not aligning with your desires. When you arrive, you'll be ready for the next destination.

CHAPTER 9

HOW DID WE GET HERE?

The getting lost is worth the coming home.

We were programmed. We live out our programs until something dramatic happens to interrupt the routines. It's not your fault; the adults charged with your care may have had the best of intentions; however, they simply didn't know the impact of their actions. Every word, event, social engagement, celebration, death, harm, and denial went into the programming of your mind.

The Bug in Our Brain constantly reminds us that we are the sum of the thoughts someone else gave us. Children have no ability to determine what is true and what is false. We develop that skill later in life when we learn there is a difference. Children watch and listen. To them, it's all truth. It's not a child's responsibility to know what is real and what is not.

For example, my wife and I told our children about Santa Claus, and if they are good, Santa would bring them presents on Christmas morning. Then, as our children grew older, the truth is revealed, and they fell to earth. I regret the moment when my wife and I told our eight-year-old son that Santa Claus was not real. We watched the joy drain from his face as he absorbed the truth. Mom and Dad lied about Santa Claus. At that moment, we vowed never again to tell our child a lie again.

Children are born with the need for validation. "I love you" is the highest form of validation we can give them. When our children succeed and we tell them "Great job" we lay another brick in their foundation of positive identity. When a child is not validated, their self-worth is lowered, and from that moment on their beliefs, emotions, and reactions to the events of life are filtered through the lens of their worthiness.

Their worthiness dictates what choices they make for the rest of their life.

Your programming dictates the choices you make today—with or without your consent.

My wife and I dedicated our lives to raising wonderful children with a high sense of self-worth. We believe we accomplished our mission. However, there were many times we questioned what we were doing. It is hard to balance the demands of young children and know if your actions are improving or lowering your child's worthiness. However, it appears they have a healthy sense of their value, and that has translated into their ability to set goals, act toward them, and handle their success.

Yet, from time to time, they still struggle with confidence. They both are much further down the road than either my wife or me. However, there seems to be a never-ending road of character and self-worth building ahead.

It's comforting to know that I'll never arrive at the "self-worth peak." I think life is to be lived. If we arrive at the destination, then the ride will be over.

Boring.

CHAPTER 10

THE CREATOR

Speak to those who are listening.

'm educated in the hard sciences—physics, mathematics, and computer sciences. I lean toward evidence-base theories and conclusions rooted in the scientific method. That said, what I am proposing in this chapter is not supported by clinical studies, scientific evidence, or research of any kind. The philosophy I present is founded in my experience and daily spiritual practices.

Why would I wander into unsupported theories and claims? Because we experience real events that cannot be measured with any human process—at least none recognized by the scientific community.

For example, I know love is real, yet I cannot measure it or prove that it exists. I experience love, and that experience shapes and molds my behaviors. It is my reality and my truth. However, the scientific community often disregards real-world evidence because it lacks a process by which it can be measured. This type of thinking—if you cannot measure it, it doesn't exist—is foolish and closes the door of imagination.

OK, enough preaching. Time for my belief system.

The world in which we live is a matrix of energy, constantly creating and destroying new forms of matter. Behind this matrix is intelligence. Some call it the mind of God; I call it The Creator, and it listens to my thoughts 24-7. No matter the name, the matrix of our existence is directed by intention, or more specifically, my desires. All living creatures have intention. Bees, trees, whales, wolves, and humans—they all move through the matrix with intention. Bees fly from flower to flower collecting pollen for

their hive, whales swim the ocean in search of food and mates, and so on. All living creatures have a predefined set of intentions including humans.

However, unlike all other creatures, humans can change their intentions beyond the basic instincts of survival and reproduction.

I believe we live in an ever-changing energy matrix that assembles, disassembles, and reassembles matter. How it assembles and reassembles the energy is beyond my comprehension; it just does.

The Creator is the spiritual ether in which we live. To me, The Creator is God, Buddha, Christ, higher power, infinite intelligence, the sun, black holes, aliens, or whatever makes you happy and comfortable. All I know is that something is working in and through me that is constantly listening to my thoughts and delivering exactly what I desire, at the level I feel I am worth.

The Creator has no judgment; it delivers what is asked of it. The Creator has no opinion or morals; it doesn't evaluate my character and determine if I am right or wrong, good or bad, a success or failure. It consistently delivers whatever I tell it I want. Like a computer, The Creator does exactly what I tell it to do based on my programming. With the benefit of time, The Creator conspires to manifest whatever I believe I deserve.

What I discovered through my own experiences was profound. It was a wickedly obvious and extremely subtle relationship between my thoughts and the world in which I operated. There are two elusive, cooperative forces that required such a leap of faith that the scientist in me simply refused to acknowledge them. I could not prove, scientifically, that the most important aspect of my discovery was the connection between my self-worth and The Creator in which we live.

The Law of Attraction is an attempt to describe the phenomena of thought impressed upon the matrix of our world; however, it lacks evidence and falls apart under the definition of a "law." Yet, my experience definitely and specifically points to a relationship between what I believe I am worthy of receiving and the experience I am having.

My journey into this belief started when I read Wallace Wattles's *The Science of Getting Rich*. This short, yet very powerful book details the theory and the prerequisites to engage The Creator fully. I recommend reading and studying his book as a component of your practice. Don't trust my word; test the theory for yourself. When coupled with higher self-worth, the evidence of this claim will overwhelm you.

Let me be clear. There is power in thought and that power expresses its desires to the Creator. It receives your intentions, backed by worthiness, and manifests your desires.

Therefore, you are getting exactly what you think you're worth, whether you want it or not. Always.

YOU CHOOSE YOUR EXPERIENCE

Climb the right ladder.

I heard a sermon by a well-meaning minister describing how God is molding his life. He said, "I am the clay on a potter's wheel and God is not done with me yet." I struggled with this idea of God's will in my life. I know I have the power of choice. The Creator gave me the ability to choose. Why would He give me choice if the outcomes of my life experiences were predetermined? That makes no sense. What does make sense is that God gave me free will and is asking me "What do you want?"

From this perspective, a new level of understanding emerges. I have free will and my free will takes the form of imagination. Imagination is the power of choice and is expressed in my actions. The higher my self-worth, the better choices I have in front of me. With better options, I exercise the one true gift God gave me: the power of choice.

As I lift my worthiness, The Creator delivers better and more meaningful opportunities. With every opportunity realized and achieved, my confidence grows and matches the next. Every opportunity is a way for me to express my desire, and my freedom of choice is how I express what I want.

Consider yourself a farmer. Your thoughts are seeds and The Creator is the ground. You have control over which seeds to plant. The Creator doesn't care if you put negative or positive seeds in the ground; it will grow them regardless. There's no right or wrong to it, and there's no morality. The Creator grows whatever you plant, that is, whatever you think you deserve.

You may ask "But I don't believe in God. Will this still work?"

Yes!

It is a universal law as valid and tangible as gravity. The scientist in me found great peace of mind and put the theory to the test many times. Heaven is what I make it. There is no hell unless I create it here, on earth.

When positive language replaces your negative thoughts, doors that appeared locked suddenly swing open. Worthy people see greater opportunities and discover pathways that were not visible before. They stand taller and feel like the world is their playground. Worthy people have purpose, dream big dreams, and have the confidence to chase them.

Remember, you are dealing with the habitual and compulsive Routine Engine. Your subconscious mind repeat thoughts, with or without your permission. Therefore, you must replace your negative self-worth weeds and plant new seeds of value. If unattended, your compulsive thinking will plant thousands of bad thoughts for every positive one. How can you expect to grow a beautiful garden when your subconscious mind is running around behind your back planting weeds?

Unless we fix the bugs in our Routine Engine, we will struggle with unfulfilled dreams and unhappy lives.

This is what I know: when clients come to me, they have a lifetime of negative thoughts growing in every corner of their life. The weeds of negative thought block out the sun they so desperately need.

We must use our Routine Engine to our advantage. We can highjack our compulsive language to plant a beautiful garden of our choosing. This is the magic of the process. We can literally brainwash ourselves with compulsive positive language.

This means you must know what you want.

What do you want?

CHAPTER 12

THE CREATOR AND OUR SUBCONSCIOUS

Ask for what you want, and know the answer is always yes.

We are dealing with a power much stronger than our conscious wants and desires. This is why we feel powerless over our habits and behaviors that limit
our success. We're dealing with the power of the subconscious mind and the habitual
nature of the Routine Engine. Most people are unaware of the thoughts and images
harbored in the subconscious mind and the power they have over our most basic of
choices. Deep within our subconscious is where our true self-image is held, and it controls the level of success it believes we are worthy of receiving.

The brain's Routine Engine is compulsive and habitual. It is built to repeat behaviors in an effort to keep you alive and ensure that your body is safe. When the brain
learns and imprints its routines, it repeats them day and night, including the thoughts
that define your identity. If you accept the fundamental premise of this theory, then
you're communicating to The Creator your self-worth 24-7. Every choice, action, and
response is governed by the Routine Engine and then communicated to The Creator.
This is why we struggle so hard and seem to be at war with ourselves. We are battling
the Routine Engine, which controls our experiences and tells The Creator what we
want. The Creator is automatic; it delivers exactly what it is told, always.

My thinking driven by the Routine Engine instructs The Creator. The quality of
the programming determines the quality of my reality. The bug in my brain is the bug
of self-worth that limits what I am able to receive, and is the same bug that communicates to The Creator.

I want good things in my life, yet I seem to be getting something different than what I want. This is the problem.

To me, God has given me a dream.

It is my job to envision my dream and communicate it to The Creator.

The Creator is always listening to the compulsive broadcast of the Routine Engine. If I tell The Creator "I'm not smart. I don't deserve a loving relationship. I hate the wealthy," I am telling The Creator I'm not smart, don't deserve a loving relationship, and don't want to be rich. The Creator responds by sending me people who make me feel dumb, treat me poorly, and ensure that wealth never makes its way to me.

Hopefully, you'll put these truths to the test. Humans rarely accept this type of information because of a book. We're creatures of experience—we want to see it in action before we do it. I get it. Try before you buy!

What I do expect is for you to test the theory for yourself. This book is a practical guide to getting what you want. It's up to you to put the exercises into practice and make your own judgment.

Self-worth is a dial on The Creator; it can be turned up or down. By turning the dial up, you tell The Creator to send good stuff. Turn the dial down, you tell The Creator to send bad stuff. It's as simple as that, nothing more. Turn self-worth up—good. Turn self-worth down—bad.

Lifting personal self-worth, in and of itself, is a huge gain for anyone. Simply having confidence in your abilities is significant. Coupled with the knowledge that The Creator automatically and purposefully responds is an equally, if not much larger, promise of serious magnitude.

In this book is The Gift. The Gift is a collection of readings, prayers, and mantras that lift self-worth. The Gift contains positive self-worth language and images that are mandatory programs for your Routine Engine. Read The Gift twice a day, for 90-days and witness the massive shift in your well-being. This is our experience with the readings. Imprint the language, images, and emotions of The Gift in your Routine Engine. Make the language of higher self-worth habitual and The Routine Engine will do the rest. The Creator will receive your new language of deserving and immediately manifest your desires. This is my experience and the experience of many, many others.

Do The Gift, and your world will change.

CHAPTER 13

UNDERSTAND WHAT IS HOLDING YOU BACK

Distracted rather than improved.

The power of our subconscious mind and its effect on The Creator are real. Much has been written and debated regarding the subconscious, and I will not argue the merits of Jung, Freud, Schelling, and countless other brilliant minds. What I know is this: when I acknowledge that my subconscious controls my life experience, I'm able to make progress toward what I want, and I stop condemning myself as weak and blaming others, including God, for my lack of success.

The Routine Engine maintains what it believes is the body's physical safety. The definition of "physical safety" ranges wildly from person to person. A committed father will have a different set of programs than a racecar driver. Both have Routine Engines, both have programming, yet both differ in choices they make.

The Routine Engine is a powerhouse. When left unaddressed, we become victims. We build Gods to thank for our good fortune and demons to blame for our downfall. We seem powerless to the will of whatever God is acting on our behalf.

For me, I was tired of losing; God had nothing to do with it. Maybe it was age or the sudden enlightenment of my being. Whatever the cause, I could no longer hide in the shadows and pretend the elephant wasn't in the room.

Every time I won, I'd plant the seeds of sabotage and start the meltdown of success over again. Sabotage occurred with or without my approval. I'd make a great move and attain success only to have it disappear, leaving me bewildered and pissed. In my younger days, I blamed the people with whom I did business. However, that doesn't take you far. Blame is a poison that others recognize (and they let you know). I listened to their advice and started owning my behavior. I stopped blaming others, but it didn't change the results. I began recognizing that my actions were causing my problems. However, I couldn't see them. I was blind. There was something else at work, holding me back.

My Coach—Bill

My life dramatically changed when I asked a friend of mine, Bill, what he was doing in his retirement. Bill said he was a coach and offered to help me. I agreed.

It didn't take long for us to discover what was holding me back. The sadness, anger, resentment, heartbreak and self-loathing that lurked below the surface of my subconscious mind scared the shit out of me. Bill and I pulled back the curtains of my psyche and found what turned out to be the treasure of my new life.

I discovered I didn't think highly of my abilities or feel worthy of the success I claimed to want. I realized I had torpedoed my success because I didn't feel worthy of receiving it. If I didn't believe I was worthy of success, then how did I expect to keep it?

Problem #1: How do I change the Routine Engine language and images to support the belief that I'm worthy of success?

While working with Bill, I studied Ernest Holmes's book *The Science of Mind* originally published in 1926. Why I liked Holmes, I don't know. I was raised Catholic and after confirmation, departed the church when I was sixteen. Holmes's theories have a strong Christian slant, and I struggled with the language (my problem, not his). I've always been a spiritual seeker and believe in a higher power, yet I never found a God I could do business with. When I read Holmes, it led me to the Law of Attraction, Law of Manifestation, and The Law of Allowing. I found Wallace Wattles' groundbreaking book, *The Science of Getting Rich*, and it launched me into the realm of new thought and metaphysics.

Remember, I'm a computer geek and have spent thirty-five years in the hard sciences. Venturing into "Woo Woo" land wasn't on the top of my list for career advancement. I practically have the scientific method tattooed on my forehead.

Suddenly, I was pulled into the dark forest of my mind.

I launched into the "Woo Woo" metaphysics of the tree huggers and naked moonlight dancers. To be sure, I was outside the scientific community I'd been a part of for decades and seriously outside of conventional religious wisdom. I was leading two lives: the world of technology (hard science) and the world of new thought (*not* hard science at all).

Problem #2: How do I put aside my preconceived ideas of what I think I know and be open to *any* answers that work?

I decided to be open to anything that enabled a breakthrough in my behaviors and moved me towards my definition of "success".

Then, one day a lightning bolt hit me. I realized that my Routine Engine was broadcasting my worthiness to The Creator at a compulsive rate! For every conscious thought I put into The Creator, there were a thousand Routine Engine thoughts transmitted with equal force. Unless the Routine Engine was aligned with what I wanted, it would win every time! No wonder I had inconsistent results with spirit, God, Christ, the Law of Attraction, The One, or quantum physics. I brought a butter knife to a gunfight.

It was clear to me what was wrong. My Routine Engine had the wrong programming. It didn't match my conscious definition of "success." That's when I realized the power of my Routine Engine and how it worked in cooperation with The Creator. I had to change the underlying programming to align with my desires *and* build the foundation of worthiness to receive the success when it arrived.

Realizing that my fundamental worthiness was low, I knew that I had to lift my deserving to receive what I consciously desired. The Creator would accept whatever broadcast I made so I better know what I want.

Bill and I focused on a Success Statement and detailed the goals and the language of self-worth required to accept it once it arrived. I began reading my Success Statement every day with conviction and emotion, seeing the results now instead of sometime in the future. With the foundation of worthiness, mixed with my desired goals, the Routine Engine accepted the Success Statement as real. The brain is pliable, and I literally rewired my neurons to accept the Success Statement as fact and critical to my survival.

Over the course of a few weeks, I instinctually and naturally focused on my goals with the confidence of a person who believed he was worthy of reaching them. I was in new territory. For the first time, I wasn't at war with myself. I found motivation where I had none, energy I never knew was available, and focus that burned like a magnifying glass in the hot desert sun.

The sudden rush of success hit me hard and knocked me off my feet. Within a few months, I could clearly see my goals and was stunned at how fast they appeared. I was pitched into a new reality, one that Henry David Thoreau perfectly captured in *Walden*:

> *If one advances confidently in the direction of his dreams, and endeavors to live the life which he has imagined, he will meet with a success unexpected in common hours.*

Unexpected in common hours was my reality. Success came at a speed I'd neither seen nor experienced. This leads to Problem #3.

Problem #3: How do I lift my worthiness fast enough to accept the abundance that is rushing at me in unexpected hours?

As it turns out, there is a limit to the amount of good I can accept. My worthiness does not increase at the speed The Creator delivers abundance. Learning how to receive abundance is the third and most critical part of your success.

For this, I needed a mentor—someone to stand next to me and coach me through the successes, not the failures. Accepting and owning my successes turned out to be a big part of the problem.

The Routine Engine compulsively and habitually communicates to The Creator my desires. However, The Creator delivers faster than I can receive it. Yes, faster than I can handle it. I have an upper limit of good and when I break through the barrier, I experience pain in the form of anxiety and fear.

Strange beasts, us humans!

In the following chapters, I discuss the problems, the solutions, and the processes you can take to change your thought patterns and the programs in your Routine Engine. The Creator will handle the rest. You can have an amazing life. I've seen this process work for thousands of people, and I know it can work for you too.

CHAPTER 14

GO WITHIN

I see what I want to see, and experience what I want to experience.
I am the creator of my world.

You are the power and create the life you live. Your world is a manifestation of your desires and what you believe you're worth receiving. When you accept this fact, great things happen. You realize that you're part of a large collective force that is constantly creating. If I'm the creator of my life, then you must be the creator of your life. That means each of us are cocreating in an infinite number of ways, mixing our self-worth in a sea of individual desires.

It's enough to make your head hurt.

If I accept that I'm the creator of my world and that my thoughts are instructing The Creator to manifest my reality, then I must be mindful of what I'm asking The Creator to do. This is where the whole metaphysical movement breaks down. Somewhere, somehow, people bought into the idea that if they desire it, it would magically show up on their doorstep. For some, this is a reality and the Law of Attraction is a reality. For most of us, the results were inconsistent.

The problem with the Law of Attraction is that it engages both the conscious and subconscious minds—specifically the good and bad programming of the Routine Engine. For those who align both minds, the Law of Attraction is real. For those who are not aware of the power of the Routine Engine, the Law of Attraction does not work and is another way for scam artists to dupe you out of your money. Believe me, I've been down that road and have made my fair share of bogus purchases. However, I believe the information in this book provides the missing link in the metaphysical field. If we don't understand the compulsive nature of our subconscious, then we believe there is another force, outside of us, acting out a series of events that we often call God's will.

God does not exist outside of you. The Creator is within and you are it. You are God and God is you. Lift your deserving so you feel worthy of answering the most important question God will ever ask you: *What do you want?*

CHAPTER 15

KNOW YOUR SELF-WORTH

All that is worthy comes at a price.

What is your self-worth setting? It's easy to determine—look around; are you experiencing what you believe you deserve? There is no magic or tricky psychological testing to determine your level of self-worth. Take inventory of your life, and determine if it is where you want to be.

Here are a few questions to help you determine where you are:

- Are you happy with your current financial situation?
- Is your relationship with your significant other where you want it to be?
- Do you experience physical well-being? Are you free of physical pain?
- Is your weight where you want it to be?
- When you look in the mirror, do you like what you see?
- Do you wear clothes that make you feel good?
- Are others treating you the way you want to be treated?
- Would your friends say you are a happy person?
- Are you close with your children?
- Do you have control over your eating habits?
- Are you current with friends and family members?
- Do you feel you have control over the events in your life?
- Do you feel worthy of owning a home?
- Is your career where you want it to be?
- Are you pursuing your life's vocation?

If you answered no to some or all of these questions, do not be discouraged. Many people are dissatisfied with what they have. You have the choice to change your Routine Engine and improve your experiences.

I removed the negative self-worth beliefs from my Routine Engine and replaced them with language and images that support what I want. It is my life long mission to change the problem areas of my Routine Engine so it aligns with what I want. Then, I naturally and instinctually make choices that give me the experiences I want.

Until this happens, you'll be at war with your Routine Engine, wondering why you're not satisfied with how your life is progressing.

It's time for new language and beliefs.

CHAPTER 16

FINDING THE BUGS

Receiving love is a difficult task.

You are receiving *exactly* what you believe you are worth. If you're dissatisfied or longing to change the status of your relationships, career, health, finances, recreation, spiritual connection, or education, there is a disconnect between your dream and what your Routine Engine is communicating to The Creator.

If you're not experiencing your dream, change what the Routine Engine is communicating. The Creator will gladly produce what is asked of it.

What's your dream?

Sara

I've known Sara for a number of years, and she had always wanted to find a great guy, get married, and be a stay-at-home mom. It was her ideal dream. One day, she expressed her frustration with me and shared how she couldn't find a good guy.

"How far are you willing to go to find the right man?" I asked.

"Whatever it takes," Sara said with resignation.

"Are you open to trying something completely different?" I asked.

"Absolutely," she responded with a touch of hope.

"Ok," I replied. "Tell me what you want in your ideal man. Be specific."

Sara and I spent an hour together in a coffee shop, detailing the specific characteristics of her ideal man. We wrote out how much he weighed, his finances and health, his spirituality, and, most importantly, how he treated her and her dream of being a stay-at-home mom.

Sara wrote a success statement, detailing every wish she wanted fulfilled in a man of her dreams, in present tense.

"Do you feel worthy of allowing your dream man into your life?" I asked.

Her response was less than confident. I suggested that she read The Gift along with her success statement. She agreed to meet me again in a few weeks to check on her progress.

Sara saw immediate results. Numerous men fitting the description of her ideal man appeared from almost out of nowhere. She went on date after date, never compromising her ideal image of the perfect man. Within weeks, the man of Sara's dreams asked her out for a date, and within 8 months they were married. She is ecstatic and knows she can get whatever she wants as long as she believes she is worthy of receiving it.

CHAPTER 17

THE COMFORT ZONE IS NOT COMFORTABLE

Surrender to the flow of good; it comes with force and purpose.

You're reading this book because something inside of you is not satisfied with how your life is going. You want to experience more. You want to be what you can be. In your mind, you hold the idea or dream of your next success. However, you feel stuck in the mire of routine that is difficult to break.

Our comfort zone is predictable. Our brain's Routine Engine impresses on The Creator our programming. The Creator is mandated to produce what is asked of it. The problem is that we must break the Routine Engine's belief and give it new programs that match what we want.

The comfort zone is the physical manifestation of your beliefs. When I say "your beliefs," I mean the life you are living right now is the direct reflection of what your subconscious beliefs are communicating to The Creator. This can be difficult to admit because life appears to be a series of uncontrolled situations and events that we seem powerless to effect. Yet there is one thing you're not powerless over and that's your attitude. You have the power to see your life in any light you wish. Therefore, your life is what you think it is and is strictly under your control.

If your life is not what you want it to be, it's because you have old thoughts and beliefs in the Routine Engine that do not match what you desire. You can change what you get by changing what you believe.

Let's take the common example of being overweight.

I spent years trying to rid myself of an extra twenty pounds. Unaware of my underlying self-worth issues, I could do little to change my eating habits and thought I could drop the weight through exercise alone. When I was young, I learned that ice cream was one of the ways my mother showed affection. I also learned that I could get my father's angry attention if I misbehaved. My Routine Engine learned that affection came through ice cream and physical pain. Until it received new instructions, I was destined to repeat the same behaviors and remain helpless to its power.

As an adult, the damage of these programs was undeniable. I became addicted to the emotional numbness of running a 10K and eating a quart of ice cream. I repeatedly pushed my body to breaking point and ended up having multiple surgeries, a hip and knee replacement, and innumerable trips to the orthopedist before I was fifty-five years old.

My brain's Routine Engine was executing an endless cycle of eating sugar and physical punishment. The need for my mother's love was delivered in the form of sugar, and the habitual physical trauma of childhood was repeated through abusive exercise routines. My comfort zone was anything but comfortable. Comfort has nothing to do with it. I was repeating what I was programmed to do. The brain is pliable and adopted the necessary routines to give the body what it needed. It would take love and affection—in any form.

When I inserted new higher self-worth programs in my Routine Engine, I stopped the physical beatings and found exercises that supported the positive treatment of my body. I still wrestle with sugar, but it's nothing like it used to be. I'm mindful of my physical body and want only the best for it.

Today, I know I'm worthy of a healthy body and act accordingly.

CHAPTER 18

HIJACK THE ROUTINE ENGINE

Choose right action over being right.

The subconscious mind is compulsive. It grabs hold of information, through routine, and bolts it into our day-to-day lives. We can hijack the subconscious mind and feed it positive information through mantras and affirmations. Once accepted, the power of the Routine Engine works on our behalf—24-7.

Affirmations work. I've used them for the last thirty years to stay sober. Religious and spiritual believers call affirmations prayers. No matter the title, affirmations are instructions to The Creator to deliver your desires—positive or negative.

Over time, the repetitive nature of your Routine Engine will communicate to The Creator your positive desires and emotions. The universal machine, in turn, sends us opportunities, and because we feel good and confident, we take action on those opportunities and achieve a higher degree of success. Once reprogrammed, the Routine Engine keeps us focused on the new destination.

For example, if you want a new home, write out the details of your dream home in your Success Statement. You do not need a vision board – with enough details the Routine Engine will fill in the details and allow you to be open to whatever The Creator sends your way. Be sure to include its location, value, size, bedrooms, and yard using present tense—as if it were already delivered. Here is an example:

New Home Success Statement

Kim and I are happy and grateful for our new home. We love walking from room to room and enjoy listening to the laughter of our children playing in our pool. We enjoy sitting under our avocado tree, drinking iced tea. We wave at great neighbors who take care of their home with the same love and attention we do. It has five bedrooms and three bathrooms and is perfect for entertaining. We are comfortable with our mortgage and are surrounded by believers and supporters of our purchase. We love our new home.

Read the Success Statement every day, out loud, for ninety days using as much positive emotion and feeling as possible. Your Routine Engine will absorb this information and make it part of its habitual and compulsive behavior. Your subconscious will naturally keep you focused on obtaining the house because it believes the house of your dreams is part of the normal routine.

This is the beauty of hijacking your Routine Engine. You stop fighting yourself and naturally and instinctually focus on only those activities that support obtaining your new home. Your subconscious is working for you instead of against you.

It is the same process the military uses to program an eighteen-year-old to be a killing machine; they call it boot camp.

We call it hijacking our Routine Engine.

CHAPTER 19

THE SUCCESS PARADOX

Success is followed by failure, resulting in the elimination of the initial success.

The Success Paradox is wired into our social conscious. "Be careful what you ask for; you just might get it!" This phrase is meant to warn us that success comes at a price and that the attainment of the goal will extract a toll higher than the success delivers.

Our experience would suggest this to be true. Over and over we see people attain wildly successful heights only to fall from said heights in equally spectacular fashion. The falls are always self-inflected. Over the years, I've had a front row seat to thousands of people attaining success in sobriety only to see them put their finger in the air as they turned and walked out.

We seem to lack the ability to handle success once it exceeds our limit—even in the smallest of amounts. Much like a car, when you drive on unfamiliar roads, your brain sounds an alarm and screams "What are you doing? I don't recognize this road!"

Everyone has this problem—from the most successful rock star to the jailed inmate. When we steer into the unfamiliar territory of abundance, success, and love, we become uncomfortable and start planting the seeds of sabotage. We humans are ill equipped to handle and accept success—in any form.

As you obtain greater and greater success, you'll feel anxiety and fear. You'll borrow problems from the future ("This will never last," or "I always screw it up") and plan for the good times to end ("When will the shoe drop?"). This is the Success Paradox. The low-self-worth voice is triggered when you drive off the road of routine. It may sound like this:

I feel guilty that I am succeeding and others are not. I'm not worthy of the abundance that so many people do not have. Why me?

This rationalization is powerful and without help is hard to get out of.

We need new programming to change the voices in our head, a coach to walk us through each success, and a safe place to try the new techniques. Once higher self-worth language and emotions are installed in our Routine Engine, we break through the barriers of success. With each new level of attainment, the Success Paradox is activated. Without help, this can be troubling times. Success does come at a price; you must learn how to live with it.

CHAPTER 20

THE RED ZONE

Over time, success always equals self-worth.

The Red Zone is the emotional space we enter when we exceed our self-worth limit. It is characterized by fear and free-floating anxiety and is the breeding ground of bad behaviors. I recall a client who came to me in desperate shape. He was on the verge of getting fired and needed to close a lot of new business or else he was done. In less than four weeks, he earned more money than he had in any month in his whole life. He was ecstatic, and on the day he deposited the check, he picked a big fight with his wife—ruining the joyous moment and success.

When asked to explain why he provoked his wife, he was clueless as to the reason. "I don't know" was all he could say. This is Red Zone behavior; it lacks explanation and often is justified or explained away as character defects, sins of the flesh, the faults of mankind, or a thousand other reasons we label human.

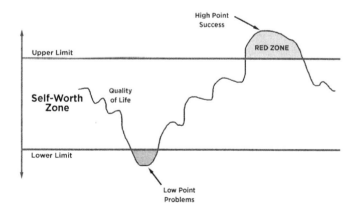

The Red Zone is an emotional state indicating the Success Paradox is active. It is when we exceed our self-worth limit as defined by our programming. Remember, the Routine Engine will constantly check to see if you're within your limits of worthiness. As soon as it detects that you're outside your limits, it triggers actions that move you back. This is the Red Zone—when your Routine Engine moves you back within your programmed limits of worth.

By the time a client makes it to me, they've burned down their house several times and are lost as to why they keep losing their winnings. They are at a loss for an explanation of their behavior. My job as a professional coach is to help them reprogram their Routine Engine, identify the Red Zone emotions, and catch the behaviors before they do significant damage.

Here's what I listen for as a coach when someone is experiencing success.

"I stopped reading The Gift."

"I am fighting a lot with my wife."

"I can't seem to get out of this funk."

"Let's go to Las Vegas and celebrate."

"My wife doesn't understand me like other woman do."

"I think I am going to change jobs."

"There is no way I'm giving my money to charity."

"They can help themselves."

"I don't have time to exercise."

"I don't need to follow up with them."

"My husband and I are fighting a lot."

"Someone else will handle those issues."

"I suck."

"Let's go out drinking."

Fill in your favorite negative self-worth saying and light the match. The Red Zone re-
lies on blaming others and finding fault in us. We're taught to avoid success because
human experience points to our inability to handle it. The reason we're not able to
handle success is because we do not feel worthy of receiving it.

I remember saying to myself, *No good deed goes unpunished.*

This is truly a self-worth-limiting statement. That's because we can't stand the
benefits of a good deed done for someone else. People who are great givers never say
this statement. They know how to receive the good of deeds done well. They know
how to live in the Red Zone of success as it relates to charity and giving.

We must learn to live with the success we attain. We know how to get success, yet
we lack the power to keep it. We must learn to accept love in all forms.

Tony

Tony dreamed of becoming a movie and television talent agent. We worked together
for six months, crafting his Success Statement and building the foundation of his self-
worth. Tony's level of self-worth was lower than most. He came to me seeking advice
as to how to make the switch from selling insurance to becoming a talent agent.

I knew I could help him succeed, but the work would all be his.

Tony found an internship at a prominent Hollywood agency and rapidly worked
his way through the ranks as an assistant to a successful agent. He was on the fast track
to his dream job and was literally surrounded by believers and supporters. Tony even
received the attention of the lead partner of the agency, something most assistants
never attain.

Then Tony missed several appointments with me. I knew that something was up.
I could feel his energy and knew he was struggling to accept the explosion of abundance in his life. Success was coming at Tony way faster than he could handle it.

He was in the Red Zone.

By the time I connected with Tony, he had sabotaged his dream job and was fired. When I asked him why he acted in such an obviously self-destructive way, he was at a loss for words. He simply didn't believe his actions would cause a problem, when in fact they were specifically the actions the firm detested. He even signed a document that prohibited such behavior.

Tony is a typical example of Red Zone behavior and the Success Paradox. The light of his success became too bright, triggered the Routine Engine, and moved him back to an emotional and physical state that matched his worthiness.

The good news is that Tony learned from this experience. He recognizes the emotions of living in the Red Zone and takes actions that enable him to retain his success. He landed another job with an even better talent agency and is making wonderful progress towards his goal.

Exercise

Tony's experience is not uncommon. Think back on your life. Where have you turned away from success or acted out in strange behaviors that sabotaged the attainment of your goals? Make a list of missed opportunities and why you didn't act or failed to change your behavior. This is an important exercise and will help you recognize the Red Zone when it happens again. And yes, it will happen again.

Everyone enters the Red Zone.

CHAPTER 21

RED ZONE BEHAVIOR

We hold the match that burned down our house.

Before discovering the power of my Routine Engine, I was a slave to my character defects. For many years I labeled myself "bad" because I lacked the muscle to change my behavior. This type of thinking kept my depressed self-worth in place by justifying how weak I was. With this programming, I'm not responsible for my actions. I fall further and further into lower self-worth as I slowly lose my strength to fight my subconscious mind. It's an endless battle that cannot be won.

For some, evil is characterized by one's lack of control over their instincts and is the work of outside forces, such as the devil. The further I fall into the seven deadly sins, the more evil I become. Ultimately, I'm an unworthy human whom only an act of God can restore. Right or wrong, thousands of years of programming have led us to the powerless conclusion that I am bad and that only an act of providence can save me.

I've never subscribed to the devil or any force outside of myself as the cause of my poor behavior. For me, the love and abundance of God is working through The Creator. It's a God I can do business with. There is only one force; it is the force of love, peace, and abundance. God's only question of me is: "What do you want?"

The subconscious mind is compulsive and reinforces what it believes. If you have self-worth issues, then negative behaviors are the Routine Engine's way of keeping you in your self-worth zone.

Every sin is an act that lowers your self-worth. Let's consider each of the deadly sins as they relate to worthiness and how they are used by the Routine Engine to maintain status quo.

Sloth

Sloth is the number-one blocker of success. It's the character defect of choice for the Routine Engine. Sloth is the reluctance to do work or to make an attempt to change a situation. For me, sloth kept me in a bad marriage for six years. I didn't think I was worthy of a loving relationship, so I attracted a partner who didn't value me or validate my needs. I lacked the ability to change and put myself first. I avoided the issue and refused to acknowledge that the marriage was broken.

The same can be said for money. We stay in poor paying jobs to reinforce your self-worth as it relates to money. Stay in the poor paying job. Sloth keeps the car in the park and hides the keys. We call it the comfort zone; yet, it is anything but comfortable.

A person who has elevated self-worth takes action and finds a job that matches their worthiness. Higher self-worth seeks greater opportunities and works to attain them. This implies we must take action – no one will take the necessary action for you. However, people who believe they are worth more naturally take action because they are worth it.

For example, take a moment and consider people you know who have high self-esteem. Are they in crappy relationships, terrible jobs, or situations that compromise their integrity? Likely not. They don't tolerate them. Even more amazing, they have the ability to keep finding better and stronger relationships with friends and family that elevate their wealth, love, and position. High self-worth takes action and is the opposite of sloth.

There are other terms we use for sloth. Avoidance, distraction (my favorite), blame, guilt, and a host of emotions that, in the end, all add up to no action.

Remember, the Success Paradox happens when you exceed your ability to accept abundance. The Routine Engine will employ sloth as its primary tool to ensure you do not move or stay in success.

Be mindful. Learn how these character defects are employed and change the language and emotional programming of your Routine Engine. Sloth will then slip away and be replaced with confident action.

Lust

Lust is a lack of self-control to restrict sexual passions. At its center, lust is the lowering of self-worth by inflicting pain on ourselves and potentially on others through sexual conduct. Lust is an outward behavior of lowering self-worth.

People who lift their self-worth have an easier time controlling their urges than those who ignore the issue. We are witness to public and private citizens who use lust as their primary tool to lower their self-worth. Over and over, both men and women pursue sexual encounters without the foundation of respect (or self-worth). Lust is a common method used to destroy a great career. Why else would someone trash their life through a sexual encounter if only to confirm their low-lying self-worth issues?

Pornography is a corrupter of self-worth. The act of viewing and engaging in pornography lowers self-worth and drives a wedge between you and your partner. Energy is lost when you act out through pornography. It can be a compulsive punishment tool for those who struggle with self-worth. It is a high sign of Red Zone emotion when pornography makes its way to your life.

Those on the path of higher self-worth manage their sexual desires. They struggle less with their instincts and don't beat themselves up when they naturally arise. High self-worth navigates the world of earthly desires by embracing them for what they are instead of seeing them as a tool of punishment. There lies the difference—using your sexual desires in a way that move you closer to your partner as opposed to using them as a weapon against yourself.

I have dramatically improved my relationship with my wife by repeating the Perfect Partner Mantra:

Perfect Partner Mantra
Kim and I have a perfect harmonious relationship that is the foundation of our family and serves as the guiding force in directing our fortune.

Kim is my wife and best friend. We've been together over twenty-seven years, and since installing the new programming, we've experienced a renaissance in our marriage. Not that it was bad before; it has always been good. However, there is something else at work. We're closer and more in love now than ever.

The Perfect Partner Mantra implies you have a "fortune" and that your love is the guiding force behind it. "Fortune" has many powerful meanings – money, success, and abundance just to name a few– all feed your definition of "fortune". Everyone has a "fortune".

Replace your partner's name in the above phrase and repeat this powerful statement over and over until it is permanent to your nature. Nothing but good comes from it.

Greed

Greed is the artificial, rapacious desire and pursuit of material possessions. In this definition, anyone who appears "greedy" is considered a sinner. How can you receive abundance and wealth and not be a sinner? This type of thinking is a loaded gun, and the trigger is the lack of self-worth. A common method of keeping your self-worth firmly in place is to label yourself a greedy person. It guarantees that you'll not achieve monetary success.

When you lift self-worth, you understand the flow of wealth and prosperity. Much like a clear mountain lake, the water that feeds the lake must also flow out. The flow of abundance must travel through you. Wealth comes to you at the speed you flow it through your life. There is no need to "hold" the wealth because it flows freely. High self-worth people are receivers and givers of currency.

The Creator flows abundance to you through money. It is the only method God has to deliver prosperity—through wealth and currency. If you're not open to receive money, then how will you influence people with your message of hope? Worthy people understand that flowing money into their businesses and then back out to other businesses is how prosperity, abundance, and wealth are delivered through The Creator and ultimately from God.

Learn these lessons. They are important.

Your Routine Engine prevents success by telling you there is a limited supply of wealth and that money must be horded. Greed is competitive and pits me against you. Greed is the seed of resentment and the birthplace of isolation. Your Routine Engine will repeat the phrase "I don't have enough" and feed your fear of financial insecurity.

At its core, your Routine Engine must be reprogrammed to flow money and prosperity. In the reading exercise The Gift, there are affirmations specifically designed to change our attitude about money. Read The Gift every day for ninety days, and watch how the flow of money and prosperity increase in your life.

Envy

Envy is a sad and restless desire toward another's traits or possessions. It disconnects me from my fellow man in a way that says "I want what you have because I don't want

what I have." A sure way to stunt my self-worth is to separate me from the human race. When I routinely envy another's traits and possessions, I am saying, "I do not like who I am and what I have." Envy enforces the false belief that if I obtain your traits or possessions, I'll feel better about myself and be happy.

Envy is the lie that promises happiness but never does.

As a race, we spend a huge amount of our time and money trying to be like someone else instead of who we are. We're a species at war with its divine self. When we elevate self-worth, we become more conscious of the greatness within us and spend less time looking beyond the four walls of our existence.

Envy is the promise that happiness is somewhere outside of us.

Envy is the Routine Engine's lever of dissatisfaction. For me, I compared my insides with your outsides and have always lost. In the race to keep up with you, happiness eluded me. Instead of turning inward, I looked to outside material possessions in an effort feel better about myself.

Use the following affirmation to come to peace with what you have.

I am whole and complete.
I am worthy of love, safety, and peace.
I love my life and the abundance that flows through me.
All areas of my life are beautiful and bright.
I am grateful for everything in my life.

It's a wonderful feeling to know there is nothing outside of you that can make you happy or sad; it's an inside job. Envy is a poison of the soul, a trick of the mind, and has no place in your practice of higher self-worth.

You are complete – now and forever.

Wrath

Wrath is anger and resentment to the point of injury or death. Most of us practice wrath in some form or another. Even now, I catch myself rehearsing imaginary conflicts while driving my car or flying in an airplane. They're absentminded arguments with people I resent or dislike. Often rehearsed, imaginary conflicts are so common that I don't even know when I am engaged in them. They are also damaging to my emotional well-being and serve to distance me from you.

As self-worth improves, we have fewer imaginary conflicts, and those that we do have, we catch sooner and are able to turn the dress rehearsal into a positive conversation.

In the end, imaginary conflicts only bring damage and pain to the holder of the resentment. Wrath is violence against my brother and sister, in any form. It is a powerful tool that keeps me away from you. Rehearsing conflict in my head never pays.

My Routine Engine uses anger to hold and fuel its position. When I have a grievance, I hold negative energy and direct it toward you. The grievance keeps me away from you and reinforces my current self-worth setting. It's as powerful as sloth.

Higher self-worth breaks free of wrath, anger, and resentment. It identifies long held grievances and works hard to clear them. By clearing grievances, we release those who we believe have harmed us and we forgive ourselves for our own actions. When lifting self-worth, we work to release our grudges. We know resentments are poison and we strive to eliminate them as soon as we become aware of their presence.

When we're free of resentments, we can look ourselves in the eye and feel good about whom we have become. In my effort to be free of all resentment, I employ the Ho'oponopono prayer whenever I discover a grievance with another human being. The Hawaiian practice of reconciliation and forgiveness clears the negative energy between me and the other party or institution. It has never failed me. Here are the steps I take to clear a grievance using the Ho'oponopono prayer:

Step 1—Find a quiet place where you can pray without being disturbed.
Step 2—Close your eyes, and envision the person with whom you have the resentment. Allow their image to appear, without controlling how it looks or the person's behavior.
Step 3—State the person's name, and repeat the following:
    "I am sorry."
    "Please forgive me."
    "Thank you."
    "I love you."

Step 4—Repeat Step 3 several times. Do not worry about getting the order of the phrases correct. It is important to state the person's name before you say the four phrases.

The Ho'oponopono prayer works because you release the negative energy of the resentment when you say *Thank you* and *I love you*, and you are taking responsibility for your actions by saying *I am sorry* and *Please forgive me*.

I have used this technique of forgiveness more than any other method. It has worked for me 100 percent of the time. I genuinely feel better when I practice it.

Gluttony

Gluttony is the practice of destroying the body and the outward reflection of internal conflict. Having been overweight for most of my adult life, I relate to this character defect more than most. As I elevated my self-worth, I naturally ate healthier foods and treated my body better. Over time, I started to value my body and treat it like a gift.

When food is scarce, gluttony is thought to indirectly kill another person through starvation. When you eat more than your share, you deprive another of food. When you leave food on your plate or throw it away, you feel the pang of guilt that you're wasting food. The pang is the Routine Engine digging in and holding tight to ancient beliefs. You don't have to travel far to see a guilty and blaming sign of starving people to lower your self-worth. It's instinctive to shame yourself for eating too much. The prison of self-worth leverages many tools to keep you in place; gluttony and the social stigma it carries are a surefire way to reinforce how you feel about yourself.

Elevate your self-worth and discover the benefit of physical well-being. The change in mental state is amazing. When you feel good about yourself, you naturally change your behaviors to support the higher image of your body.

I recite the following mantra from *The Master Key System* by Charles F. Haanel. It centers me and helps me know that my body is exactly as it should be. Repeat it until it is ingrained in your Routine Engine and becomes habitual.

I am whole, perfect, strong, powerful, loving, harmonious, and happy.

Ego

Ego is a negative virtue that changes the human faculties to be more like God and is thought to be the source of the other deadly sins. This is a slippery slope; one could argue that this whole book is precisely a sin of ego (false pride) by questioning the nature of God.

So be it.

In the context of this book, the ego is the display of lower self-worth. True pride is an amazing emotion, yet without gratitude, the feeling of pride looks more like arrogance. Pride mixed with worthiness is magic and very attractive. It takes the form of high self-esteem where confidence and worthiness are matched.

Ego is bombastic and flashy; it's the lack of gratitude. It's the outward display of low self-worth that is so present in our society today. "Look at me!" is as common as eating or drinking.

Real success reinforces your pride in a job well done. It builds confidence, which motivates you to go after another higher goal. Raising your self-worth broadens your vision and lifts your goals, your understanding, and your true pride.

Don't confuse pride and with ego. Pride is built on a strong foundation of self-worth and is balanced with humility and gratitude. Ego lacks self-worth and is bolstered with loud and pompous displays in an effort to gain recognition. Pride does not need recognition from without, only from within.

Higher self-worth builds pride.

CHAPTER 22

THE LIMITING ROUTINE OF SELF-WORTH

Low self-worth is the root of all bad behavior.

Self-worth is compulsive and a habit enforced by your Routine Engine. Much like ruts in a road, we become accustomed to how the road feels. When we drive off the road and enter the Red Zone, we ache with anxiety because the Routine Engine doesn't recognize the road.

Consider driving a car for the first time. For me, I learned on a stick shift. Operating the clutch, accelerator, brake, steering wheel, blinkers, and other instruments while avoiding traffic and navigating the road was scary and complicated. When I first learned to drive, my dad was in the front seat, telling me what to do, and if he spoke too quickly or shouted directions, I'd lose my focus and get confused. The safety alarm sounded in my head, and I got scared.

However, after six months of driving, my dad and I could have a conversation about my schoolwork while I easily drove the car. The emotions, language, and physical routines of driving were in my Routine Engine. I'd driven my car at least ninety times, and the behaviors were now considered a safe routine. My subconscious mind accepted the behavior, learned it, and it was now a subconscious act.

This is the power of our Routine Engine.

As a child, I had many "you're not valued" experiences. Even though the daily routines of my childhood where physically and verbally unsafe, my Routine Engine figured out how to navigate the world and survive. Safe routines were developed and reinforced over the years. The early routines kept me safe, and I knew how to get away when things got bad.

Today, the same routines form the foundation of my decisions. When presented with an opportunity to ask for a raise, my Routine Engine filters the information and generates the response "No, this is not safe." Unable to ask for what I want, I kick myself and lower my self-worth.

Sound familiar? What I've discovered through hundreds of direct coaching experiences is that every person has some degree of old safety routines that limit them and their attainment of success. Safety routines keep us from asking for what we want and prevent us from accepting gifts laid at our feet.

The purpose of this book is to provide a practical guide to lifting your self-worth.

The voice that blocks me from taking action is the voice of safety, and it goes something like this:

I'm safe here; overweight, eating sugar, and in a crappy job. It is not safe to exercise, eat smart, or interview for a better job. Besides, no one protected me, gave me encouragement, or paid any attention to me. I'm broken and broken people stay broken. I don't deserve a fit body, good food, or a better job.

Here's the good news: we can change the voices. This book leverages techniques that I've personally found effective at clearing the problem images that threaten our self-worth and replacing them with the strong, self-empowering voice of deserving.

You may ask, "How do I know that I'm stuck in a low self-worth routine?"

Take inventory of your life. Are you getting what you want? If not, worthiness and the programming of your subconscious are restricting your success in that area of your life.

For example, if you have a low paying job, then the Routine Engine believes you deserve a low paying job, otherwise you would have a higher paying job. The example may appear too simple, but it is not. You receive what you believe you're worth, nothing more or less. Lift your worthiness and have a better experience. People who believe they are worthy of more, get more.

Once your brain accepts new language and emotions as safe, the Routine Engine absorbs the programming and applies the routines in your daily life. Deviate from the set routines and anxiety kicks in and tells you "This is not safe." We must allow the routines of success to lock in and allow your self-worth to rise to the new level of worthiness.

This is how you change your life.

CHAPTER 23

HANDLING THE FLOW OF GOOD

Gratitude helps me keep wanting what I have achieved.

Your foundation of self-worth was programmed when you were a child and slightly modified over the years. Depending on your parent's moral code, abilities, prejudices, experiences, and a host of other conditions, you developed a self-worth identity that defines exactly how much good you will allow into your life. That is, there's a valve controlling the flow of good, and your worthiness turns the handle to increase or decrease the abundance you receive.

Let's be clear, the level of deserving is not set by your conscious mind. Every single person I meet would accept more money—a lot more! The problem is that our Routine Engine is significantly more powerful than our conscious mind, and on top of that, the Routine Engine is compulsive. Once it accepts a routine it believes is important to the well-being of your body, it imprints the routine and repeats it over and over.

Unless you are mindful of your Routine Engine, The Creator will deliver exactly what you believe you deserve—despite your intention to do otherwise. It is the only consistent explanation for why people do stupid things once they attain even the smallest amount of success.

When you accept the premise that all your choices are driven by self-worth, there is real hope for a permanent change in your life. The day your Routine Engine believes you deserve a beachfront home will be the day you'll act compulsively to make that dream home a reality. Moreover, your Routine Engine will communicate to The

Creator your desire for a beachfront home and arrange the people and opportunities necessary to bring the dream to reality.

Practice The Gift, and the Routine Engine will accept it as fact.

After ninety days, the Routine Engine will accept The Gift as truth and will repeat the positive emotion and language habitually. Your Routine Engine will repeat these positive statements when you sleep, when you drive, and when you eat. They'll press out the negative thoughts of lower self-worth and will take the dominant position in your thinking.

Read The Gift every day. From time to time, you'll notice a voice in your head saying *I don't need to read The Gift today*. This is *exactly* when you need to read it. The voice will say, *Ignore the readings. I don't need to do that stupid crap.* This is the voice of old programming, with the bugs, of your Routine Engine. It's the scared voice of your programming, resisting change.

Self-worth reinforces its position. It works to hold its ground by spreading anxiety and fear by telling you the new position is unsafe. Here are a few standard Routine Engine bugs meant to hold you back:

What if...
...I fail and people laugh at me?
...I make more money than my parents?"
...I succeed? I don't know how to handle money."
...I'm not smart enough?"
...I make others feel bad because I succeed?"
...Someone finds out that I am doing this woo-woo stuff?"
...I look stupid?"
...I make a fool of myself?"
...I fail?

It can be hard handling the flow of good in our lives. Most people would rather complain about how bad their situation is rather than do something about it. My friends and I have a saying that separates the victims from the accountable.

Complain more than three times and you're just looking for attention.

Blame is a powerful addiction and is a programming bug that truly restricts our ability to break free of our limitations. Blame is the victim's drug of choice. A strong foundation of self-worth frees us from blame and allows us to see the world for what it is: a creative space that is always listening for what we want.

CHAPTER 24

LIVING IN THE RED ZONE

The business of listening is always profitable.

The Red Zone is the emotional state I enter when I exceed my upper limit of what I believe I deserve. When looking for indications of the Red Zone, procrastination and rationalization are the leaders of the pack. For me, I lose focus and get distracted.

No amount of personal planners, motivational seminars, and time management systems are going to fix the problem of focus and procrastination. The problem is worthiness and the limiting language in my Routine Engine. Red Zone behaviors are warning signs that I'm about to screw up my success. When I change the language and emotions in my Routine Engine, I naturally find the energy to focus and take action while I am in the Red Zone.

With each new level of success come newer, more exciting goals. Every time you exceed your Routine Engine's programmed limits and enter the Red Zone, new bugs are exposed. For me, I consider the newly exposed bugs as gifts. I learn more about myself and how I relate to you when I live in the Red Zone.

Therefore, for those who want to succeed, living in the Red Zone is a normal way of life. It is uncomfortable on purpose. It requires the support of a professional coach who can see what you cannot. Living in the Red Zone is hard without help and leads to actions that most people are not equipped to handle alone. The Routine Engine is too powerful. We need help.

This is why I founded Motive For Life, a professional coaching company dedicated to changing the world, one dream at a time. We focus on lifting our clients' self-worth and walking them through the challenging process of living in the Red Zone. It's exciting and fun and a way of life I personally never dreamed possible.

Living in the Red Zone is an amazing place to be. It is exciting, thrilling, and scary—all at the same time.

"What if I can't afford to hire a coach? Is there anything I can do to help my success?" you may ask.

Yes, I've outlined a set of Practices in this book. Most are easy to implement, and you should see immediate results. However, I've witnessed many who have made the Practices a routine in their lives without a coach, only to quit two weeks into the program. They enter the Red Zone, unaware of the emotional impact of living above their worthiness limits, and think the Practices are not working. They stop the behaviors that moved them toward their goals only to have their Routine Engine overpower them and stop the progress.

Team up with others who are walking the same path. Lean on each other, meet weekly, and build accountability into your practice. Let others know when you're in the Red Zone so they can keep an eye out for sabotage behaviors.

As you improve your worthiness, be mindful of the Red Zone. Awareness is the key to success.

PART 2

THE BUGS

CHAPTER 25

CIRCUMSTANCE RATHER THAN VIRTUE

To pain we obey.

The practice of building self-worth is driven by two forces: pain and desire. Although we want to believe it is virtue that elevates our identity, humans rarely change unless there is a fire of consequence combined with the wanting of a higher quality of life, be it wealth, happiness, or love.

I'm certain you didn't wake up this morning and say "I'm going to buy this book and follow its recommendations and become an individual of higher self-worth." More likely, you woke up and said "I'm tired of losing, and I can't take this anymore." For me, the red-hot flame of circumstances forced me into a corner, looking for a way out.

I know how it feels. Crushed under the debris of my choices, I had nowhere to turn and no one left to blame. Only then did I become teachable. It seems to be our nature. Beaten by the results of our actions, we're forced to do something different. We can choose to get angry or we can choose to see it as a gift.

Comfort does not advance us. Hopefully you have an inner voice dying to get out and be heard. It says:

I'm tired of losing! There has to be more to life than this. I want to do something else, but don't know what it is or dare try.

Therefore, it's the circumstances of your life, not virtue, that have driven you to this point. I hope the pain you're in is sufficient enough for you to take action. If not, put this book down and turn on the voice of procrastination and justification.

Pain is the great motivator. It takes the form of unfulfilled dreams and keeps us moving forward, striving for a greater realization of desire. There are those who, at the end of the day, seem to have a built-in desire to do better. At times, I envy those who naturally build on their success. Yet, for most of us, and probably for you as well, it's the pain of our current situation that has driven us to this point.

It's OK to want a better life—more money, stronger relationships, more respect from your colleagues and peers. God's judgment of your faults and failed aspirations are another's burden. You want to strive for a better life and the realization of a purpose, a dream. Maybe it is the pain of not being able to put your kids through college, or the unfulfilled dream of earning $100,000 a year. There are an infinite number of reasons we want to strive. My wish for you is that you move from the circumstances of your life and start dreaming of what you want.

I'm OK with that. I hope you are too.

People who understand the power of self-worth recognize what drives them. There's a joy in knowing what moves you forward.

I'm motivated by my desire for a better life. There is ownership in my human truth, driven by inspiration and imagination. Money makes my life better. Money makes the lives of those I employ better. Wealth makes life better for those who receive my tithing. I make the world better for those who are willing to flow money from my companies to their companies.

I know what money does. Cash improves the quality of life.

However, money without happiness is hell. It amplifies our pain by removing the obstacles of daily survival. The pursuit of wealth is noble when self-worth rises to meet it. Worthy and deserving people understand that money doesn't bring happiness, yet they know the power it does bring to their family and community. Both happiness and wealth can and do coexist. Therefore, we can take solace in knowing our human desires for comfort are balanced with our deeper need for happiness.

Own who you are and what drives you. Listen to the voice within and believe you're worthy of the gift it has waiting for you.

CHAPTER 26

BE YOUR OWN BEST FRIEND

When offered a gift, say yes.

The transition from external to internal is uncomfortable. Most of us are programmed to look outside of ourselves for reasons why we're not getting what we want. When we change our programming and lift our worthiness, we turn inward, look at the obstacles within, and strive to remove the language, emotions, and images that block our success.

Without a doubt, you must be your own best friend.

If you recorded the voices in your head and then played them back for others, would they agree you're your own best friend? If you're not your biggest fan, then who is?

For me, I could never predict how I felt about myself. There were days I'd wake up, look myself in the eyes, and could not see any beauty at all. There was no apparent reason for my uneasiness; I felt at odds with myself. I didn't understand the power of the Routine Engine and how it habitually repeated negative phrases and emotions. Like a flawed program in a computer, it repeated the same code unaware of the effects it produced. The bug usually showed up late at night while I slept and left me with an emotional hangover in the morning.

The language and emotions we use to talk to ourselves defines our self-worth and set our level of confidence. Worthiness and confidence form self-esteem. Self-esteem is a person's overall evaluation of his or her own worth. Most of us can easily recognize individuals with high self-esteem. They're like the sun; we want to orbit them and live near their warmth. Good things happen when we're close to those with high self-esteem.

Negative language and emotions alienate others by generating negative energy. It's hard to be your own best friend when you constantly repeat language that holds you back. Consider these self-sabotaging phrases:

"I'm not good enough to do that."
"I'm so stupid."
"They're better than me."
"I can't ask her out. She would never go for a guy like me."
"I'm not pretty enough."
"My face is ugly."
"I wish I had her butt."
"My hair is ugly."
"I never graduated from college."
"I don't make enough money."
"Why did I do that?"
"I wish I never said that."
"Why do they hate me?"

There are an infinite number of self-sabotaging phrases. However, there is one phrase that tops them all.

"If only..."

The phrase "If only" is followed by a regret. *"If only I said the right words, she would like me."* "If only" covers every possible angle of lower self-worth. The emotion of "if only" includes other self-demoting phrases such as "would have," "could have," and "should have."

"Would have," "could have," and "should have" is an addiction and the language of a victim. It is the whip of regret with which we flog ourselves for decisions that didn't turn out to meet our expectations. Victims use "would have," "could have," and "should have" so frequently that it's embedded in their psyche and is habitual.

"Would have," "could have," and "should have" is common language used to re-gurgitate an experience for the sole purpose of punishment. Instead of letting our words stand, we compulsively replay the experience with the subtitles "*I would have…I could have…I should have…*"

Here are a few examples:

"I should have saved for my retirement sooner."
"I would go back to school if I had the money."
"I should have said something to that man when he insulted me."
"I should have asked for that promotion when I had the chance."
"I could have been a better parent."
"I would be in a better relationship if I wasn't overweight."
"I could have done better_____ (Fill in the blank)."

You must be your own best friend; no one is more qualified or more important than you for this role. The exercises in this book are designed to replace "would have," "could have," and "should have" with self-worth raising language, emotions, and images. The Gift works for those who take the action.

CHAPTER 27

CHANGE THE STORY

The answers lay submerged in the dark waters of the soul.

How do we change a painful story?

The default answer is forgiveness. We must stop feeling angry or resentful toward those who harm us. Much has been written about forgiveness, and there are many paths to the top of that mountain.

For me, forgiveness wasn't enough. Yes, I released those who had harmed me. As a recovered alcoholic, the discharge of resentments is a mandatory process. I'm free of anger toward those who held power over me. Yet, there was something left hanging around, picking at my psyche like a woodpecker hammering on a tree.

I was left with the tattoo of lower self-worth. Forgiveness of others does make me feel better and does raise my self-worth, yet the emotional scars of traumatic events significantly change how I view myself. Forgiveness does nothing to repair my damaged identity. My Routine Engine captured the events and used them as a filter for every choice I made, and if a choice fell outside of what I deserved, it triggered anxiety to maintain the status quo.

I needed to replace the painful stories in my Routine Engine.

The Locker Room

When I was twelve, I was beaten with an oak paddle I made in woodshop class. The backs of my thighs and calves were covered in dark blue bruises. While in the locker room of my seventh-grade PE class, a teacher saw the injuries and asked what had happened. I lied. I said I crashed my motorcycle while riding in the desert. I knew the

PE teacher didn't believe me, but without my cooperation, he could do little. He left to attend to other tasks as I got dressed. I tucked the event under my skin and held it here for decades.

Oddly, I remember the time when the teacher discovered my bruises—not the beating itself. The discovery of the beating held much more power over me than the actual event. I felt deep shame that someone knew what had happened. I remember the compassionate looks of the PE teacher, the fluorescent locker-room lights, and the military green wood benches. It is strange how the brain works.

I held this story in my mind's eye for decades, reliving it over and over, pulling it out when it served a purpose. On the surface, if asked to repeat it, I would downplay the event. I revisited the locker-room trauma several times with counselors and close friends. I had long "forgiven" my offender and was living out my life as any normal adult male.

In reality, I was a man with a wounded child identity, and it manifested itself in the form of self-abuse. Initially I drank and took drugs to blot out how I felt about myself. When the drugs and alcohol stopped working, I had to face reality and do something about it. I cleared a great deal of wreckage and healed many of my wounds. However, my damaged self-image never was addressed.

Recovered alcoholics have lost the ability to turn off their thinking through drugs and alcohol. Physical exercise was my new drug, and I exercised to injury on a recurring basis. I literally tried to run away from myself.

There were two forces at work inside me. The first was the need to turn off the self-hate voices and the second was the pathology of physical abuse. I had to feel pain to feel love.

For many years, long distance running, biking, softball, and hockey distracted my mind from me. It was like digging a hole in the sand on the beach. With every shovelful I lifted out, more sand rolled in. Over the years, I got tired of shoveling. There had to be another way. My life was OK, but there was so much more to experience, and I wanted to be free.

I wanted to be happy when I wasn't trying to be happy.

I know there are people who are happy all the time. I married one.

My locker room story needed energy to stay alive. Without the energy of my attention, the negative stories of my life would die from neglect.

I keep my stories alive by feeding them energy and allowing the troubling events to be remembered. Literally, by keeping the story going—telling others, thinking about it, rehashing it—The Creator manifests the events through actors whose job it is to fulfill their parts. With each reenactment of the story, I fed The Creator, and it recreated the scene: the abusive authority figure, the sympathetic but powerless friend, and me the helpless child. As long as I held on to the event, I was guaranteed to relive it.

I needed a new story.

However, the Routine Engine held tight to the images and emotions of that event. How was I to change my story when the Routine Engine held so firm?

The Routine Engine needed another story to replace the one it held. That meant I needed to construct the new images, language, and emotions of how I wanted to remember the locker room.

I wanted to be released of the pain and receive the love. Instead of the PE teacher finding me in the gym with bruises, I changed my memory of that school day.

New Locker Room Story

My dad drives me to school, puts his hand on my shoulder, and says, "I'm proud of you, son." I run off to class, smiling. I joke and play around with the other boys in the locker room, laughing and talking about girls, knowing that when I get home, my father will take me to baseball practice. I close my eyes and see the scene, feel his hand on my shoulder, smiling at me like only a father can smile at his son. I feel a deep sense of love, value, and confidence. I repeat the scene, over and over, in my mind's eye. I resolve never to relive the trauma of the locker room and release the guilt I know my attacker would feel having hurt a child.

I installed the new memory in my Routine Engine and made it habitual. I only speak of the locker room and the PE coach when the memory serves a purpose (such as this book), otherwise I embrace only the memories I want.

I've sought out painful events and replaced them with memories that support a loving and brilliant childhood. With each new story came the release of blame and the elevation of self-worth. Funny thing about this process: new people are showing up who are completely different from the ones I used to meet. Now I meet happy people with fantastic lives and big dreams.

Search your memories and decide which ones need to be replaced. If you want a new relationship with your family, friends, and colleagues, envision what you want and create the new story. See the new story as real and in the present moment. Repeat the scenes, language, and emotions until your Routine Engine accepts them.

It doesn't matter that the events never happened. Memories are energy, and if you're going to expend energy, then you may as well make the energy serve you.

CHAPTER 28

FEELING GOOD IS DIFFICULT

Real change happens when there is something at risk.

Why do we spend so much time criticizing ourselves?
I stare into a mirror, look at the size of my stomach, and wish I looked differently. I replay scenes of failure and disappointment over and over in my head with little attention to the pollution I feed my mind. I've spent endless days, weeks, months, and even years talking negatively to myself, rehearsing imaginary conflicts, and nursing unresolved grudges.

Why do we spend our time bringing ourselves down?

Feeling "less than" is an amazing fact of our nature. Women try to outdo each other's problems, and men complain endlessly about their jobs and the burden they wish they could change. There are hundreds of channels of bad news media, blaming others for our problems. The emotional addiction of wounded self-worth is global. We spend endless hours and money trying to change our emotional state, and we don't seem to be making much progress.

We don't feel worthy of the blessings we've attained.

The problem is bigger than you know. We don't like who we are, and the addiction to verbal and emotional self-abuse is systemic. Why else would we complain so vigorously about topics that are out of our control?

The subconscious mind is compulsive. It will repeat thoughts over and over, much like a song stuck in your head. The subconscious mind is always chewing on images and ideas and never stops in its compulsive behavior. It's the foundation of the Routine Engine and never stops.

I grew up in a violent household. Most days nothing happened; however, there were days that drained any storehouse of self-worth. The repetitive nature of these thoughts and images controlled my worthiness. No amount of forgiveness of others' behaviors improved how I felt about myself. The Routine Engine programming was set to the following language and belief: *I didn't deserve protection—not then and not now.*

As a father, I understand a child's desire for safety and validation. I can still hear my children's voices calling for our attention:

> *"Daddy, look at me. Daddy, watch me. Daddy, I can do this. Mommy, look at me swim. Look at me!"*

A child is constantly seeking validation and appreciation, and when they don't get it, their self-worth suffers. It is imprinted in their programming and reinforced by their Routine Engine.

When I was young, my parents and the sum of my experiences set my level of self-worth. As an adult, I consistently and habitually replay my imprinted stories.

> *"I'm not good. I can't do it. No one appreciates me, so why try.*
> *Every time I try to do something, it doesn't work out."*

Over and over, I reinforced my self-worth through the language and images in my subconscious mind. Moreover, it was happening at a level of thought I was unaware of.

There is a solution. It's in this book.

Those who have done the work are living amazing, productive, and successful lives. They are living their bliss because they believe they're worth living their bliss.

I'm here as a living testament that self-worth can change. You can lift it up and have a new experience as a result of higher self-worth. More importantly, you define what success means to you. No longer are you restricted to the definition of "success" given to you by well-meaning friends and family. When you learn how to align your thinking to get what you want, only you restrict what is possible.

Happiness is the reality of what I believe and know is true. Once you have overcome the barriers of self-worth, you too can recover and have a glorious life that equals your dreams.

CHAPTER 29

UNDERSTANDING THE BATTLE

Your opinion of yourself is the learned voice of others.

Mary and Joe work at a factory, loading products into boxes. Their duties and hours are the same. They receive the same pay; however, Joe hates his job. The other employees complain that he is hard to be around and constantly blames the supervisor for his crappy work experience. Mary believes in the company and wants to be a manager. She has a positive attitude and is promoted within a month to a supervisor position. Both Mary and Joe have identical job experience, yet Joe is frustrated and eventually quits while Mary is promoted.

Why? Because Joe's thinking is different than Mary's. Joe has self-worth problems, and Mary feels worthy of success.

What haunts Joe is the battle between his conscious desires (family, safety, money, success) and his attitude towards the world (lack, anger, unfulfilled desires). For Joe, it's hard to see wealth in the face of poverty. How can Joe imagine success when he is struggling to pay the rent? Joe is lost in the disillusion of his anger and frustration, never pausing to consider that his attitude is the problem. Until Joe takes ownership of his thinking, he'll never get out of the cycle of blame and low self-worth.

We relate to Joe because we all suffer from the same thinking. The power of the subconscious mind and the Routine Engine is enormous. It rules and governs all our experiences. Without knowing what bugs lurk in our programming, we're tormented and plagued by circumstances that appear out of our control, and we never feel the warmth of true success.

We must learn how to access our programming and take action to change it. The mind is clay and can be shaped.

Without a doubt, changing our thinking is a challenging task. It's not for the weak of heart as it requires a sincere desire to look at the past and a willingness to correct our thinking as it relates to others and us. A change in attitude is required to make progress. People are not willing to take these steps unless they have hit an emotional bottom.

Every person I've had the privileged of helping has had one common theme: they want to start winning. Here are three examples of people who have completely changed their lives. They had a change in attitude and thinking that launched them on a course of action.

- A failed adolescent and hardened drug addict, in and out of jail, now holds a successful sales and marketing position (for over two years), where the owner of the company often tells him to stop selling because they cannot keep up. He has more money than he knows what to do with. He gives freely.
- An insurance salesman had a struggling business. He examined his beliefs and discovered that his whole childhood was about being let down by his father. He learned that he surrounded himself with people who let him down. Today, he is crushing it because he was fearless in his desire to find the root of his limiting beliefs and remove the obstacles that blocked his success.
- A navy officer and MBA grad struggled with his management-consulting business, never finding solid ground by which he could launch his professional services company. In a few short months, he is activity involved with several start-ups and changing the lives of many people.

If you don't have the desire to clear your obstacles, success is likely to be temporary. The Routine Engine will return you to where it believes you belong. It is powerful and always wins.

"But what about my terrible childhood? How do I unwind this mess?" you ask.

I totally understand. I held the belief I was trapped in the routine of anger and regret.

However, I know that the subconscious mind accepts the highest dominant thought as real and with repetition, accepts *any* language and emotion into the

Routine Engine. Given ninety days of repetition, morning and night, the subconscious mind will internalize the thought and repeat it to The Creator for manifestation. It does not matter if you believe in this process. Powerful men have brainwashed other men for centuries. This is not a new technology. If you want change, set out to brain-wash yourself with what you want. Much better that you control what is in your brain rather than others.

No one can manufacture your desire to change. You must find it yourself and hold on to that desire as if your life depended on it.

"I am worthy" drives you to achieve more. You are more alive, more joyous, more abundant, more giving in all areas of your life.

You are what your deepest desire demands.

CHAPTER 30

AS I SEE ME, I SEE YOU

You are my brother and sister. The love of life is lifting you up.

Why do I criticize others? I find the voice of judgment always by my side. It is ever present, creating differences between you and me, justifying my behavior as better than yours, and pretending that you and I are not alike. In truth, I am you, and you are me. My judgment of you is my judgment of me.

How I see me is how I see you.

I used to judge overweight people and call them weak. In reality, I didn't like my body. Every time I looked at myself in the mirror, I gripped my stomach with both hands, condemned my fat gut, and wished I had the discipline to eat better. My judgment of you was my judgment of myself.

I had a wounded self-image of my body; I didn't like how I looked.

When I accept my body for exactly the way it is, I see people who struggle with weight for who they are: people, the same as me. With each boost of my self-worth, my negative views of overweight people drop because I do not have a negative view of myself.

Judgment is the mirror of my value and is a cage of my belief. The bars of the cage are reinforced by the words I tell myself. I hold you in the same cage as I hold myself.

The evidence of my freedom is in the language I used to describe others. If I talk behind your back and spread rumors or gossip, I'm living in the cage. However, if I speak with compassion for someone I disagreed with, I know I have increased my self-worth and am flying free of the cage.

Listen to your language. Do you gossip, judge, or criticize people for any reason? Do you find yourself engaged in negative or disruptive discussions involving politics,

business matters, or world affairs? Do you have resentment toward a colleague, and make fun of them in a business setting under the disguise of a joke?

Your true self-worth is always on display. Change how you see yourself and the judgment of others will slip away.

My Dad

When I was thirty, I decided I wanted the best possible relationship I could have with my dad. Deep down, I wanted him to tell me he loved me, to say the words out loud, and mean it. I am worthy of his love.

My grandmother on my father's side was as affectionate as a rattlesnake. Her mother, my great-grandmother, had five husbands. All of them died while they were married to great-grandmother. Low self-worth flows through my family's veins. More impressive is the fact that they willed themselves to a comfortable level of economic and social status. They definitely were not happy; however, they did establish themselves nicely in the middle class.

At the time, my mentor was Tony Fisher. Tony was an awesome man and possessed great skill at navigating difficult and wounded relationships. I told him I wanted to hear "I love you" from my dad. He said, "Then let it start with you."

That wasn't what I wanted to hear.

Yet, in classic Tony form, he laid out a course of action that proved brilliant in its nature. I would teach my father how to love. In turn, I would receive what I so desperately desired.

It started with a hug.

Hugs are leading indicators of self-worth. Watch people who hug and those who are being hugged. A hug is an overt expression of love and typically from someone who has a healthy balance of self-worth. My dad always greeted me with a handshake. "How are you doing son?" he would say. "Fine," I'd reply.

Nothing special and definitely not the relationship I wanted.

Under Tony's direction, I changed how I greeted my father. At first, it was extremely awkward. Instead of a handshake, I put both arms around him and squeezed. You'd have thought I was infected with Ebola by my dad's reaction. He froze, held his breath, and tried to wiggle free. My dad made no attempt to hug back.

During this time of my life, all I could think about was my childhood. I didn't understand the relationship between self-worth and how I lived my life. I just wanted a relationship with my dad that was more than superficial. Now I understand. I didn't get what I needed, and it wasn't his fault. No one taught him how to love, so how was he to love me?

Over the years, I took every opportunity to hug my dad. Initially, he responded with a stiff back and an awkward grunt. He realized I wasn't going to stop and caved into my advances by the fourth or fifth encounter. Within a few months he was giving me the one arm man backslap. Hang around men and you'll see this pseudo macho move all the time. As a group, men don't like to hug for fear we'll catch some nastiness. My dad was no exception. He maintained a slight distance, slapped me on the back, and considered the whole "love fest" over.

What happened a year or so later was massive and nothing less than a miracle. I began to notice he expected a hug. Although the embrace was not what I wanted, he was changing. When we met, he came in for the hug, albeit short and stiff, and embraced me with higher energy. He smiled and lingered more before releasing me. There was a shift. At the time, I didn't know what had happened, but now, as I look back, I lifted his self-worth by teaching him how to love me.

Self-worth is powerful. When I showed my dad love, I lifted his worthiness.

It was magical.

Yet, with all the progress we were making, he still hadn't said "I love you."

Tony said, "When was the last time you said it to him?"

Never. I was guilty of the sin I wanted fixed in my dad.

The thought of saying "I love you" to my dad filled me with fear. With each social event, the anticipation of saying those three killer words raised my pulse and backed me into a corner. How could I expect my father to say "I love you" when I lacked the courage to do it myself?

The day came when I had no choice. It was Father's Day and the pressure of my unexpressed love could not be held back any longer. As my family approached my parents' house, my dad opened the door. "Hey bud," he said and came in for a hug.

We embraced and I said, "Happy Father's Day Dad. I love you."

Nothing. He turned and walked back into the house.

No fireworks, no parade, no "I love you too, son."

The day passed easily. I felt good for having taken the step and busted through the emotional barrier.

My dad had pretty much stopped drinking around me when I got sober. He is exceptionally mindful of my alcoholism and supports me in his own way. However, that Father's Day he had a few.

As we embraced and said our goodbyes, he hugged me and said, "I love you."

Drunk or otherwise, I took it! I held the words like a mother holds her newborn child. To this day, I still sense his difficulty in saying "I love you." I cherished the effort, even if it took several drinks to release its grip.

I say "I love you" to my dad regularly; however, it would be another ten years before I would hear it again from him. Strangely, he said it just prior to the publication of this book. It was clear, purposeful, and heartfelt.

He's trying, and I love him for it.

Thank you, Dad.

CHAPTER 31

THINK IT IS REAL, AND IT IS

Perception is the law governing experience.

Perception is reality. For example, when I have a disagreement with my wife, the root of the situation is always perception; she sees the problem differently than I do. The only way the conflict is resolved is when someone changes his or her perception of the problem. Therefore, perception is always reality. How I see me is how I see you. The perception of myself is always reflected in you.

If you regret your past, you'll relive it every day and make decisions filtered through the lens of your regret.

If your boss is a jerk, then ask yourself "Why do I allow myself to be treated poorly?" If your response is "I need the money," I totally understand and appreciate that reasoning. It is a totally acceptable answer; however, what changes are you making to your self-worth that ensure you'll never work for a jerk again? If you're not taking action to leave, then you may have an issue with worthiness.

We all have choices. Yet, many of us don't understand how self-worth defines our perception of the world and how it shapes the choices we make.

In my life, I've made decisions to work with people I knew would end badly. There were plenty of red flags. My perception painted them green, and I proceeded anyway.

Why would I consciously choose to work with someone I don't like? The standard answer is "I needed the money." However, I now know that answer to be a lie.

My other mind, the Routine Engine, is in control and forms the basis for all my choices. I had the illusion of control and thought I was making logical and sound choices. However, my Routine Engine is significantly stronger, more consistent, and

more compulsive than any willpower I could muster. It made sure I returned to bad relationships.

The good news is that we can change the Routine Engine and gain new and fresh perspectives on life. With the bright light of our new perception, we are able to make better choices that are in alignment with our goals.

Your perception governs your decisions. Change how you see the world for the better and your experiences in this world will change with it.

CHAPTER 32

WORTHINESS DRIVES OUR CHOICES

Saying yes to good is hard and the core of the issue.

Every decision we make is based on our level of worthiness. We've the ability to choose behaviors that benefit our well-being or hinder our progress toward our goals. Yet, we simply find it hard to do the right thing consistently. We make poor choices and beat ourselves up over our lack of power and then chastise the image in the mirror for being flawed.

Prior to any decision, the Routine Engine receives the input, runs the decision through its logic, and makes a choice based on its current programming. Let's consider an example from my own life.

I struggle with eating snacks late at night. Logically, I know that eating chips at 10:00 p.m. is unhealthy. There are days, however, when I simply block out the logic and go straight to the cabinet and pull down a bag of Fritos. It's like I'm a drone being piloted by a foreign power with the objective to make me fat. Halfway through the bag of salty goodness I realize what I've done and launch the negative voice of condemnation.

This is the Routine Engine at work. My childhood programming associates late-night snacking with affection. My mother loved to snack at night, and we often shared happy times together over a bowl of ice cream or a bucket of popcorn. Snacking at night is self-sabotage and a Red Zone behavior. When I'm feeling good about myself, late-night snacking goes up.

"Why would the late night snacking go up when you're feeling good about yourself?" you ask.

When I exceed my worthiness, I enter the Red Zone and the Success Paradox kicks in. I am feeling better than I deserve. The Routine Engine draws from its programming and pulls me back to old and destructive behaviors. This is why I feel powerless over my life. The Routine Engine is compulsive and habitual and moves me in ways I do not see.

The evaluation of self-worth is rapid and precedes the act of choice. By elevating our worthiness of wealth, health, love, and success, we instinctually make better choices without wasting energy fighting the initial decision.

How you think about yourself drives the decisions you make. Every action you take is a decision based on how the Routine Engine determines your worth. The higher your worthiness, the better your choices.

CHAPTER 33

THE NEED TO BREATHE

We pay more attention to what we put on our feet than what we put in our head.

We must honor our deepest desires otherwise we live a schizophrenic life. We can minimize the importance of wealth, security, passion, and love for only so long. Heck, we can go through life making excuses that conform with social, political, and religious beliefs, but at the end of the day, we cannot hide from our deepest desires.

I've made countless excuses for not following my dreams. In reality, all I'm doing is holding my breath and pretending that I don't need to breathe. Eventually I'm going to need to take a breath and honor myself.

Look around—the world is full of people not breathing.

For me, I was told the road to a better life was to help others. The cure for selfishness and self-centered thinking is to help someone else. Service work provides relief for a short period of time; however, the relief is not permanent. You can't give away something you don't have. We must clean up our own backyard before we can help others clean up theirs.

Time to focus your attention on your needs.

You must honor and lift yourself up and breathe. You can go without water for three or four days. You can go without food for about thirty, but you can't go more than about three minutes without breathing. As far as I'm concerned, your self-worth is as vital to life as breathing air.

Let's start breathing. Look at yourself in the mirror and say the following:

I love every part of my body.
I love my stomach.
I love my butt.
I love my face.
I love my eyes.
I love my hair.
I love you.

I'm bald, so I say, "I love my bald head."

Affirmations work.

In church, we called them prayers. There is no difference. Affirmations are prayers—prayers are heard by The Creator and The Creator answers *yes*. Every word we speak is a prayer; every word is heard.

You are a temple. Every part of your existence needs to breathe.

You can hold your breath as long as you can, but in the end, you'll need to breathe.

CHAPTER 34

YOUR BEST THINKING
GOT YOU HERE

The Queen rules the kingdom she built.

No matter how you slice it, your thinking brought you to this point. If you're reading this book, you're looking for a change and probably not a small one. This book is for those who've accepted that they are responsible for their choices. They know their life is in their hands and the choices they made placed them in the position they're in right now.

Stop blaming others for how your life turned out. Move from a helpless passenger to the driver of your success. Stop complaining about the state of affairs in your country, community, or family. Let go of blaming others for your career, debt, marriage, and children. Stop being a victim, and realize that you're in control of your life—from this day forward.

Blame is a seductive partner. Blame is the avenue of zero accountability and is the blood brother of low self-worth. Blame lowers confidence, which reinforces limiting beliefs. Here are a few blame phrases we use every day:

"I can't because I have a low paying job."
"I need to have a degree this before I can make a $100,000 a year."
"I couldn't move because of my wife."
"I don't have money because I lost my job."
"I quit because the boss was an asshole."
"If only..."

"You make me feel bad."
"You don't understand what she did to me."
"They did this to me."
"He made me feel bad."
"It's too late to late to change my career."
"I'm too old, young, stupid, broken, little, big, fat, skinny, ugly, strong, black, white, girly, wimpy...on and on."

You can change your self-worth by practicing the readings and exercises detailed at the end of this book. Victim language is a symptom of worthiness issues, not the cause of low self-worth. Own the fact that you've acted and behaved like a victim. When you take ownership of this fact, progress happens and you're set free.

Those who advance their self-worth take ownership of their lives, know that they direct the show, and feel worthy of the applause.

CHAPTER 35

ALL ALONE, BEING RIGHT

We live the external manifestation of our internal reality.

As you lift your self-worth, your desire to be right rapidly disappears. People who insist on making their point lack the self-worth of owning their position on a topic. Confidence is powerful and doesn't need to convince others that it is right or wrong; confidence just exists. Higher self-worth people know that their opinion on a topic could be different tomorrow and are willing to listen to truth when it appears. Therefore, they rarely insist on being right.

Stunted self-worth insists on being right. When we're unwilling to listen to another's point of view, we isolate ourselves from the human race. Isolation is a primary method of lowering self-worth.

The more power we invest in our point of view, the lonelier we become. Loneliness is painful. The more willing we are to listen to other people's points of view, the more we feel connected to the rest of the world. It doesn't mean we have to believe what others believe. We're willing to listen to what others have to say, and to allow them to say it, allow them to believe it, and allow them to have their own point of view.

There's a lot of respect in allowing others the freedom to speak their truth. The higher our self-worth, the more willing we are to listen to another's point of view. We have more compassion for people. We can hear the self-worth issues in other people's language and have compassion for their struggle. No matter their beliefs or desires, we recognize their journey and allow them to walk their path.

Higher self-worth allows others their experience without judgment. This is a goal, and for me, something I wish to accomplish. However, I still have a few bugs of

separation in my Routine Engine that manifest themselves in judgmental thoughts about others.

However, when I am able to connect with you, there's the natural effect of lifting me up and connecting me with you. I can then accept you for exactly who you are, and at the end of the day, I end up accepting me for exactly who I am.

When I allow other people to be who they are, it actually allows me to be me, with all my faults, with all my challenges. I am like everybody else, and they are like me.

People who understand the power of higher self-worth make room for everyone.

CHAPTER 36

THE QUALITY OF OUR CONSCIOUSNESS

All is flowing to wellbeing.

I'm no longer a victim of my thinking. The more aware I am of my thoughts, the better my opportunity to change how I see the world. Understanding my thinking requires me to observe my thinking. Meditation helps me identify my positive and negative thoughts, and make a choice as to which ones I want to pursue.

Imagine your thoughts are cars on a road. For the purposes of this story, the cars heading north are positive thoughts and the cars heading south are negative thoughts. Meditation enables me to watch the traffic of my thinking and identify which thoughts are heading north and which ones are heading south. I choose to be in the cars heading north. I like positive emotions and want to increase the frequency of thoughts that lift my self-worth. The practice of meditating enables me to identify my thoughts, label them, and decide which ones I want to entertain.

If I find myself indulging in negative thought, I can change it. Consider the following painful narrative:

I should have saved more money for retirement.

This thought doesn't serve me. I'd rather be thinking of ways to increase my earnings, not engage in punishing voices of regret.

Meditation helps me stop and change the direction of my thinking. This is a very powerful tool. I can catch my thoughts going in a negative direction and literally stop

and say, *No. I choose not to travel in this direction. I choose to travel in the opposite direction, in a positive way.*

The results are undeniable. When confronted with a troubling situation, I have time to respond to the input as opposed to reacting. I'm able to stop my downward spiral thinking. More importantly, I'm in a positive mood where I can take steps to help the situation and improve my outlook on life.

For many, meditating is difficult. It takes practice and a sincere desire to improve the condition of our thinking. Combined with the other exercises in this book, it creates a platform of self-worth that is unshakable.

The goal is to have a flow of positive self-talk so you don't have to monitor your emotional temperature. The Routine Engine is simple and pliable. You can change the programming and patch the code. When your internal voice is one of encouragement, love, and happiness, the world rushes in with massive gifts.

This is the power of the practice. Replace the bugs in your brain with positive language that attracts new and better opportunities. And because we have higher self-worth, we have the confidence to pursue them.

Your success is preordained.

CHAPTER 37

THE LANGUAGE OF THE HEART MUST BE HEARD

Success eludes those who know their liabilities better than their assets.

To bring out our best, we must listen to and speak from our heart. We are naturally drawn to strong people with high self-esteem. The higher our self-worth, the more transparent we become. The more transparent we become, the more we let others know what we desire. When we let others know what we desire, the world turns to deliver it to us.

Those walking the road of higher self-worth are confident in their conviction, are not concerned with what others think about them, and attract people who support them at every step. They are clear with their beliefs. They communicate what they want. They say, "Here I am. I am authentic and love every aspect of myself—all of it."

As a public speaker, I must speak from my heart to reach the audience. When I am transparent with my stories, emotions, and beliefs, I gain the support of those who sing the same songs as I. The more I let you into my heart, the more I am supported.

Activity

Record a video of yourself describing a person who is important to you. Tell the story of your favorite memory and why you love them so much. For me, my first mentor was Tony Fisher. Tony was an amazing man, and he absolutely knew how to reach me in ways that no one else could. He lifted me up and gave me strength when I had none. I keep a picture of him on my desk while I write.

Practice talking about somebody you love. Listen to the language. If it's true and authentic, it's coming from your heart. People will recognize it and draw closer to you for being transparent. The more you can expose your true self, the more people will want to be around you. Believers and supporters surround and gravitate toward those who lift self-worth.

Send the video to the subject of your short speech. They will love it.

CHAPTER 38

THOSE WORTHY OF SUCCESS, KEEP IT

The washing machine does not care how the clothes are loaded.
In the end, they always come out the same.

Buried in the dirt are the jewels of your success; rough and uncut, they carry the power to change your life forever. You must dig in the dirt and find them, otherwise you are restless and without purpose.

I recall the saying "Be careful what you ask for; you just might get it." Even the sages knew the attainment of success came with a price. The price is self-inflicted; it's the pain of exceeding our self-worth limits.

Humans have a hard time handling good. We lose our minds when success rushes into our lives too fast. The punishment of exceeding our threshold of good may come in many forms, but one thing is for certain: we get very uncomfortable with the attainment of success. History demonstrates that we don't know how to handle our success, so we are taught not to ask for "what we want" lest you be looked upon as foolish. We are trained to deny our dreams because the evidence suggests that we don't know how to handle it once achieved.

I was raised Catholic. I am reminded of a phrase the priest said before communion.

Lord, I'm not worthy to receive you but only say the word and I shall be healed.

I ran in the opposite direction of the church when I was sixteen. For years, this phrase held no meaning for me. However, while writing this book, the phrase would not leave

me alone. Over and over I helplessly played and replayed the communion scene in my mind's eye. Then it hit me like a lightning bolt on a clear summer day. I understood what the ancients were saying.

"God, I am not worthy to receive you…" means I don't know how to handle the abundance you're sending me. The abundance of the universe is too much for me to handle!

"…but only say the word…" means say the *right* words, the words of higher self-worth. I am love, I am wealthy, I am healthy, I am good.

"…and I shall be healed." Yes, say the right words and I am healed of my inability to accept the flow of good in my life. If I say the right words, heaven will flow to me now. I will be worthy to receive God's abundance because I am healed.

This is the beautiful connection between worthiness, language, and God.

It is time to dig in the ground and find a belief that works for you.

Prayer works. Prayer is asking for what you want. Man has been praying since the dawn of time, asking God for help. Those who feel worthy of asking for specific help, get it.

The question is this: What are your prayers? What are you asking for?

Since every word you speak is a petition of The Creator, you better know what you want and then have the worthiness to keep it once it arrives.

When I ask people what they want, they stutter, look confused, and say "I don't know."

Actually, they do know what they want but lack the confidence to say it. They've been taught to keep their desires - quiet lest someone call them greedy.

Asking for what you want, when done in a good way, puts you in touch with the infinite. I've witnessed cancer disappear, sickness removed, wounds healed and miracles delivered. When asked with faith of self-worth, the Creator always says yes.

Then why do we avoid asking for the necessities of life? Why can't we pray for prosperity, strength, harmony, abundance, wealth, healing, and love? Why do we save prayer for emergencies or the knowledge of God's will?

The reason is clear. We are punishing creatures and have come to believe that asking for what we want leads to the downfall and pain of man. Since God always delivers beyond our worthiness, we act out in bad ways and burn down the gift. Without

knowledge of how the system works, our only conclusion is that God is punishing us
or asking for selfish desires.

Here's the prevailing logic:

Ask God for what I want.
God always delivers beyond what I can handle.
Pain follows because I don't feel worthy of receiving the abundance.
Sabotage my life through character flaws and poor behavior.
I experience the pain of losing.
Lesson: Don't ask God for what I want. Only ask for the knowledge of His will.
You will not be disappointed with what you get because it must be God's will
and He knows better.

Here's an alternative. Proposed new logic:

Ask God for what I want.
The Creator happily delivers.
God always delivers beyond what I can handle.
Elevate my self-worth to handle my new level of abundance.
Watch for Red Zone behaviors and stop them before I can sabotage my results.
Allow the abundance to settle into my life.
Feel great and loved by God.
Do it again.

The way to get what you want is to be worthy of it. The more worth you have, the
faster the gifts arrive.

CHAPTER 39

WE MUST BE WHAT WE CAN BE

Worthiness precedes a life of purpose.

People who feel worthy of success are those who want to know their purpose. They know there is a path and it is beautiful and bright. When they follow their purpose, they feel wonderful, motivated, and connected.

As we search for our personal truth and mission, there are fewer and fewer places to hide. Eventually, we must face the real possibility of what we must become. For every success, another peak appears and our imagination is lit again. With each goal attained, with each success accomplished, we see more clearly and another magnificent horizon appears.

With each breakthrough of our upper limit of self-worth, we get closer to knowing what we're to do while on this planet. For many, breaking through our upper limit triggers alarms in our head, saying "Warning! You're approaching your dream." When this happens, a heat wave of fear rises up and tries to keep us from our greatest experience.

For many, the light of success is too bright.

Once you recognize the road signs and the emotional discomfort of living your dream, you cannot turn away and pretend it doesn't exist. You must live and embrace the journey you are on. Recognizing the emotions of success requires practice and, for some, the assistance of a professional coach.

For me, anxiety and fear are the lead emotions that surface when I'm breaking through an upper limit. Procrastination is the most common behavior. I ignore what it is that I'm to do next and I'm distracted by shiny objects.

I've come to recognize these road signs in my life They say, "Robert, you're nearing nother barrier of what you believe you're worth." When this happens, I take action nd reinforce the language of self-worth, love, and abundance by reading The Gift and ny Success Statement. It settles me down. Occasionally, abundance and love arrives aster than my ability to accept it; it outpaces me. I call my coach, walk it through, and am able to absorb the new order.

This is a practice; we must learn how to accept abundance.

With higher self-worth, we can face the challenges of success. Winning in life is a natter of accepting it and being worthy of keeping it. So often we see people winning t life only to sabotage the success and tear it down.

If you've decided to lift your self-worth, then you can no longer avoid your des-iny. All the hiding places have disappeared, and you must squarely face the beauty of our life.

There's no place left to hide.

CHAPTER 40

THE TRUTH IS ALWAYS WAITING TO BE HEARD

Truth desires comfort and seeks a companion.

Those who seek higher self-worth are those who seek the truth. They want to know what is holding them back and how to remove it.

Truth is ever present and waiting to be discovered. It's as if we are surrounded by it—hiding in plain sight. For those seeking higher self-worth, there are moments of clarity when the truth rushes in and fills the empty chambers of our soul. Learning the truth about us can be a difficult process. We may want to know some truths, while others are better left alone until we are able to face them.

For those who are seekers, the quest for truth is in the forefront of our minds.

All the lessons of time are here; they knock at the door and wait for us to let them in. They're ever present. If we open our eyes, the truth is there. If we open our soul, the truth will flow in.

Beautiful times follow the recognition of truth. We must know that our highs and lows are necessary. We cannot avoid the advancement of our being. We must become one with it.

Each time we elevate our worthiness, we open the valve of abundance to even greater opportunities. We have clarity of vision because we're open to seeing the truth. The teacher is available at all times and everywhere. Our readiness comes with a willingness to understand that there are greater truths to be heard and we're worthy to hear them.

Those who walk the path are those who want to hear the truth.

They demand the truth.

CHAPTER 41

FEWER WORDS

State your convictions openly, for without a face, they ring hollow.

As we lift our self-worth, the need to be heard softens as we make our point briefly. We spend less time trying to convince others of our point of view and more time lifting them up. We speak to those who are listening and focus our intentions. The most powerful people in the world speak with the fewest words.

When self-worth is lifted, our need to be heard dies; we speak less and listen more. When we listen, we learn how to connect with others. The practice of listening turns us inside out, and we see the ropes that hold us back.

When I listen to you, I give you love, grace and a space to have your point of view. The fewer words I speak, the more space I create for you to connect with me. This lifts my self-worth because I allow the connection to happen between us.

I also give myself the opportunity to listen to my own voice. I draw people to me who like my energy, and when they speak to me, they express what I truly feel about myself. This effect can be difficult to recognize, but as you elevate your worthiness, you'll see how beneficial this tool can be.

For example, if someone at my office is negative, resentful, or distrusting toward me, I must acknowledge this person as a mirror of my own internal voice—specifically, my internal self-worth meter. I ask myself, *What negative, resentful, or distrusting energy is within me that has drawn this person into awareness?* If I am willing to answer this question, then I am able to make a shift within myself that reduces conflict with my sisters and brothers.

Those worthy of their success listen more and speak less. They know the people they meet are the reflection of their inner dialog. By listening to others, they discover the bugs in their brain.

CHAPTER 42

EXPERIENCE WHAT YOU WANT

Pink cloud or stormy skies · what's your choice to be?

Lifting self-worth changes how you see the world. The higher your self-worth, the rosier the world appears.

Perception shapes the view of my world. How I see you and how you see me are dictated by the filters of our perception. Self-worth is the primary yardstick by which I judge my actions and is the keystone of my understanding. Worthiness is like a thermostat; it sets the temperature of my condition and controls the level of my success. When I change how I feel about me, the outside world changes accordingly.

Changing how I feel about me is not easy.

Layer upon layer of conscious and subconscious thought are habitually repeated in our mind. The Routine Engine is constantly working and runs the programs it was given. As humans, we've spent thousands of years trying to tame and gain control over our urges. Our core values, supported by language and emotion, are the framework of our perception. If we see ourselves as unworthy, we'll judge every situation through the eyes of an undeserving person and turn away great opportunities and avoid the right action.

The programming happened when we're young and had no ability to determine what was true or false. At a time when we need the truth more than ever, we're fed our guardians' truth, and the mold is cast.

Seeing our world is seeing our worthiness. If we loathe the wealthy, our self-worth thermostat is set too low when it comes to money. We must turn up the deserving of money, or else we'll never have riches. Wealth brings impact and influence. Worthy people know the power of money and use it to lift the collective well-being of the planet.

For example, if you distrust men, then men who are liars and cheats will surround you. You've set your self-worth thermostat to attract men who betray you. The wound of betrayal is in the Routine Engine and broadcasts the energy of betrayal to those who have the need to betray another. The bond of energy is then connected, and the Routine Engine works until the betrayal occurs, completing its programming.

You may ask, "How do I trust another man?"

Worthy people see what they want to see. That is, they hold the image of a good man, an honest man, in their mind and download the language and emotions into their Routine Engine so they align with their higher goals.

To experience what you want takes effort. You must find the language, emotion, and images that are holding you back. Seek out what is blocking you and insert new programs that match your desires. This process may require a coach to help you write a Success Statement that supports your goals. Once written, read it out loud, every day, for at least ninety days. This is the download process required to imprint your wishes in your Routine Engine.

By lifting your self-worth, you can see what you want to see and experience what you want to experience. You will change your perception of the world. When you change your perception, you change your reality.

It's an inside job.

CHAPTER 43

IT'S NOT ME YOU WANT

The foundation of great decision-making is the elevation of self-worth.

We follow the taillights of those who lead the way—mentors, coaches, gurus, yogis, priests, pastors, motivators, and teachers. We need people who know what they want and how to get it. They become our closest and most trusted advisors, and sometimes, we put them on pedestals.

I attend retreats several times a year. I frequently attended one in Santa Ynez, California, at a Catholic Franciscan Hermitage where the brothers are the finest example of acceptance I've ever encountered. We typically host fifty alcoholic men at the monastery; tattoos, unrestrained anger, bad language, and a genuine dislike for any organized religion make for an interesting mixture of cigarettes, spiritual awakenings, and nasty storytelling. Surprisingly, nothing serious ever happened in over twenty-five years of retreats. The power of retreats bond men and women together like no other process. This is why I established the CDM Retreat Center, a nonprofit charity dedicated to sending men and women to retreats while they're still early in sobriety. We have found that retreats are key to extending the length of sobriety, and the sooner we can get to them to a retreat, the better.

I was raised Catholic and departed the church some time ago, not for anything the church had done to me; all my experiences with the cloth were wonderful. I departed because my dad never went to service and my mother always made me go. In a fit of rebellion, I told my mom I was not going and that was that. Today, I occasionally sit through a mass; the routine is strangely comforting but that is as far as I am able to go.

At the retreats, I became friends with Father Gerald, a silver-haired Irishman who made me feel good about who I was and what I believed. He never condemned me for walking away from the church, and to this day, I love him for it.

Father Gerald had a way of putting things together. I remember discussing with him why people put others on a pedestal. Specifically, I was getting a lot of requests for my time to help men get sober. I was pulled in many directions and was confused as to how much time I should spend with them. I had a family, little kids, a career, wife, and mortgage. I wanted to help but lacked balance in my service work.

Father Gerald told me, "It's not you they want, Robert. They want what's inside you."

His words struck me hard.

He continued, "I serve my community in their highest joy and their worst pain. They want me to pray for family, to solve problems in their relationships, to bless their babies and bring salvation when they die. They want me all the time."

He paused, looked away as if thinking about a painful moment, and said, "What I realized, it's not me they want. People don't want the faucet. They want the water that flows from it."

We sat quietly, listening to the soft spring breeze whistle through the pine trees. It's not me the men want. They want what shines in me, the light of hope that they too can change their life. They want what I've found and want to know how they can find it too.

My ego had stepped in and was enjoying center stage.

I thank Father Gerald for his wise words.

People with solid self-worth flow their joy and happiness. They flow the clear waters of life through them, never taking credit for the source.

People want the light that is inside you. They want the essence, the being, and the energy that ignites the fire of hope. Bring out the light, that light of value, that light of love. Bring it to the surface so all can see it.

NEVER REGRET A DECISION, EVER

The past is lost to the present.

With each new level of self-worth come brighter colors of confidence—the kind of confidence that builds upon itself, like layers of cement in the foundation of your life. Those who practice building their self-worth are those who rarely look back on decisions with judgment. That's because once a decision is made, there is nothing they can do to change the past; it is done. No regrets. They make the right choice every time. If better information were available prior to their choice, they would have chosen differently.

You have the power to view every one of your choices as perfect. Only you have the ability to judge them differently. Why choose to view your choices as bad? If you need to reverse or change a decision, do it. That is another perfect choice. Therefore, all your decisions are perfect.

This mind-set frees you from bad thinking and the abuse of "would have, could have, and should have." Regret causes pain and questioning your decisions is a habitual behavior to keep you in pain. Free yourself from regret and make the choice to change how you think about your decisions. This surprisingly simple, but not easy, decision is at the core of our success. Imagine, making perfect decisions that lead to your success? How wonderful would life be if you could look at each choice, knowing that it was perfect, and know that the next choice is going to be perfect as well?

You have this power. Only you can choose to celebrate or condemn your behavior—no one else. When you say "Wow, I make great choices," you set the stage for all future actions and behaviors. Trust fills your being, and your self-worth rises like the tide; nothing can stop it, and it floods your world with confidence.

People who work to lift their self-worth rarely spend time questioning their decisions. They say, "Well, perhaps I could've made a different choice. However, I didn't know what I know now. Next time, I will choose differently."

You may ask, "There are decisions I know I need to make, like pay the rent, but instead I gamble the money away at a local casino. How is this a good decision?"

In this situation, you are dealing with the bugs in your programming. The Routine Engine has taken control and is holding you in your zone of worthiness. Your desire to pay your rent lacks the power to override The Routine Engine. Instead, you cash your check and head to the tables.

"So how is this a perfect decision?" you inquire.

Good question. It's perfect if the decision has led you to the point of dramatic change. No human has ever made substantial progress without first encountering the pain of the current situation.

I didn't get sober because I wanted to be a better man. I got sober because the pain of my existence was too unbearable; I couldn't endure one more day as a drunk. I hit bottom, which enabled me to change and look for a solution. Therefore, every decision I've made as a drunk was perfect because it led me to massive healing and the healing of many others. The gold in my life is my ability to look at my experiences and know that they were necessary.

Start with reading The Gift. The language, emotions, and images of the readings will begin the imprinting of higher self-worth in your Routine Engine. You'll naturally make decisions that are in your best interest and feel less guilt and remorse over decisions that lower self-worth. It takes work and effort to practice The Gift every day; however, it is worth it, and you're worth it.

Regret is the pain of the past. Regret is a weapon used by the Routine Engine to keep our self-worth shallow. Our memories and negative feelings about ourselves are strong and are difficult to release. By changing the language we use to describe our choices, we free ourselves from the grip of regret.

Practice The Gift, get a coach, and align your Routine Engine with your desires.

It's a wonderful way to live.

CHAPTER 45

THE BURDEN OF DEBT

The punishment will continue until worthiness is lifted.

For many, the path to higher self-worth means the attainment of financial freedom. Debt is often part of the problem. We see and want financial security yet our actions are not in line with our goals. We know debt doesn't build financial freedom; however, we still acquire more of it. Millions of us spend money we don't have. We build a mountain of debt and create crushing stress that only serves to lower our self-worth.

We're not stupid; we know debt is bad, but we spend money we don't have anyway. We reinforce our limited self-worth every time we think about the money we are wasting on abusive credit-card interest.

Look at the statistics from the US Federal Reserve for 2016:

	Total owed by average U.S. household carrying this type of debt	Total debt owed by U.S. consumers
Credit cards	$16,061	$747 billion
Mortgages	$172,806	$8.35 trillion
Auto loans	$28,535	$1.14 trillion
Student loans	$49,042	$1.28 trillion
Any type of debt	$132,529	$12.35 trillion

The numbers are staggering. We have buried ourselves under a mountain of debt.

Why? Debt is the opposite of financial freedom. We're putting the chains on ourselves, not taking them off.

Worthy people strive to limit debt as much as possible. For me, this was the last frontier. I had the most difficulties clearing my credit-card debt. It was a real struggle and for reasons that were not obvious at all to me.

I remember the day when I looked at my bank account and realized I had enough cash to pay off all my debt. As a matter of fact, I had had enough cash to clear my debt for some time. Why had I not paid it off sooner? The question rattled in my head like a metal bolt in a clothes dryer. What hold did credit-card debt have on me?

Then it dawned on me; I used credit-card debt as the primary whip to flog myself. The primary regret story of my subconscious mind was "Look at the debt; you suck." Because my subconscious mind is habitual, it repeated this statement a hundred times a day. With each look at the card balance, I added another nail to my retirement coffin. And because I have a low self-worth image, it reinforced that I'm not worthy of financial freedom and success.

My wife and I agreed to pay everything off and never to acquire credit-card debt again. We even had a ceremony when we paid off the cards. We both held the mouse, navigated to the part of the website, and together clicked the Pay Full Amount button.

What a great feeling. We blasted through our self-worth zone, and it felt wonderful. However, the joy didn't last.

Strangely, I felt uncomfortable and anxious. My number-one go-to self-worth story was gone. I was free, but I didn't know how to handle the good emotions of success and happiness. I struggled with the positive emotions of being debt free. And apparently, so does most of the population.

We, as a society, are addicted to pain. We need to feel bad.

The need for financial insecurity overrides our conscious mind and seems to force us to make poor choices. Financial security is not safe in the mind of a person who struggles with self-worth.

After thirty years of working with alcoholics and drug addicts, one common theme surfaces like an iceberg: alcoholics have extremely low self-worth, and nothing makes an alcoholic thirstier than success. Alcoholics rely heavily on "would have—could have—should have" to justify their misfortune and blame others and themselves for their plight. Financial insecurity is the leading problem for the newly sober; very few arrive at the doors of recovery without financial wreckage. It is our most common weapon of punishment.

Alcoholics are extreme cases, but their solutions also work for people who don' have addiction problems. This is the good news. No matter who you are, what you'v done, where you live, or what you do, there is a solution. We can lift our self-worth an gain control over our lives.

"Would have—could have—should have" is self-abuse talk. Resign from the "self hate" team, and make a conscious decision that all your decisions are perfect, includ ing your past spending habits. The great discovery is that when we lift our self-worth the flow of success and prosperity enters our lives.

We have plenty of time to build our financial freedom. Money comes in way faster than expected when we stop resisting the flow of good in our lives. This is my experi ence as well as the experience of many, many others.

If you're like me and want to change how you feel about yourself, then The Gif will make a big difference regarding your financial well-being. It contains an affirma tion regarding prosperity and sets you on the road to recovery. It is very powerful anc has helped many people.

CHAPTER 46

TRUST ME, TRUST YOU

Confidence is rooted in the belief that I am worthy of success and the belief that it will be so.

We practice elevating self-worth. It's a life-long endeavor that pays returns far greater than the initial investment. Trust is the result of higher self-worth. We know we'll follow through with our commitments; we develop muscles we never knew existed. We trust ourself naturally, and it comes with ease.

To not trust oneself is a living hell. The alcoholic is an extreme example of someone who has lost all trust in his abilities to control and enjoy his drinking. He breaks promise after promise to those he loves, and most importantly, to himself. At its very core, this endless cycle of broken promises is the continuous lowering of self-worth. Not only is the alcoholic physically addicted to booze, he's mentally addicted to the punishment inflicted by repetitive broken promises to himself.

The solutions in this book are not obvious to the average person. To assert that worthiness is the root of your problems is a big leap of faith. However, when the exercises and readings are implemented, you'll trust others because you'll trust yourself.

As you rise in self-worth, the level of trust others extend to you will rise. They will confide in you more, trust you with more personal information, and will let you into their lives at a deeper level.

Worthy people can be trusted. They are included in bigger deals, asked to participate in great business opportunities, lead incredible teams and build wonderful companies.

People trust people who trust themselves.

THE BAD NEWS

Many ask for help but do nothing to take it.

As you lift your self-worth, you'll recognize that the human race is addicted t pain. We live in a habitual world of mental punishment, and our primary tool bad news. Bad news is the heroin of our times. The flow of negative emotional energy piped through every media device is the needle delivering the drug. We read, argue sympathize, fight, lament, comfort, and grieve the pains of people we don't know, i places we've never seen, for reasons we don't understand.

Breaking the addiction to negative emotion is hard. Consider a presidential elec tion and the twenty-four-hour news cycle. It's a relentless barrage of character thrash ing at an international scale. Media outlets gorge on the advertising revenue and pra for a tight race. It's insane, and we love it.

There is a price: the price of happiness. Time to stop the madness and move to ward our center.

Turn off all news media and commercial advertisements that don't lift your self worth. The DVR is the perfect self-worth builder. With social media, unfollow anyon who posts negative language, makes fun of or builds up a class of people at the ex pense of others.

For me, airports are the hardest place to avoid the bad news. There are moni tors in every corner blasting the bad news while waiting to board a flight. The world airports have news channels with a large portion of the screen dedicated to the two second reader. It is a banner, approximately six to ten words, briefly describing th most recent bad news. It is impossible to avoid.

Some airports have the volume turned up so loud that I have no place to hide from the bad news. Headphones are a start but could cause me to miss a flight if I don't hear an announcement. I seek out quiet spots in airports so I can protect my mind. I have a passport to free thinking, and I intend to use it.

You may ask "How will you know what's going on in the world?"

I disconnected years ago. Since then, there have been two presidential elections, two wars, multiple terrorist bombings, murders, rapes, gun-control battles, health-care reform, and a sea of "Did you hear about…" (fill in your latest bad news).

Here's what I found. I can come in and out of the bad news under my own control. I determine when I want to engage the media. I determine how much I can handle and from whom I receive my pain. I protect the portals of my mind because I know the words I hear and the images I see affect my happiness.

Pay attention to your own well-being. Protecting the portals of my mind is a top priority. Be careful of what you allow in your brain. You'll feel better not knowing who shot, attacked, invaded, blasted, crushed, or took over whom.

Don't invite new bugs into your head. Protect your brain and be careful of what it consumes; you want to control the programs in your Routine Engine.

What news do I read or watch?

Sports. I love the athletic mind. Professional athletes are great examples of focused thinking and the heights they can achieve. Most days, it's a fun read.

Turn off the bad news and protect your mind.

CHAPTER 48

AT WAR WITH OUR HIGHER SELF

We're not bad people trying to get better; we're good people trying to get out.

Every choice we make is motivated by how we see ourselves. If our worthiness is high, our decisions are better, and in turn, we receive better results. If our worthiness is low, we make poor choices that result in bad outcomes. Many people believe that luck or the will of God controls the outcomes of their lives. However, there is considerable evidence that our choices absolutely define the quality of our lives. Luck, God's will, chance…these are paper tigers used to deflect personal accountability and owning the outcomes of our decisions.

Worthiness is directly related to the size of our character defects (or our sins—if the word works better for you).

Greed, sloth, lust, gluttony, anger, envy, and pride all balloon with lower self-worth.

The lower our worthiness, the more crippling our character defects. Greed leads to stealing, sloth to depression, lust to rape, gluttony to obesity, anger to violence, envy to war, and pride leads to isolation and death. All our choices are driven by our worthiness.

If we believe we are worthy of a healthy body, we instinctually eat right, exercise, and take care of our body. If we make right choices that support a healthy lifestyle, we can expect good results. Those who lift their self-worth are people who maintain a healthy lifestyle because they know they deserve it. Period. No other reason.

Those who wrestle with self-worth swing dramatically in all directions when it comes to physical exercise. For me, I exercised until my body fell apart. I played football, baseball, and wrestled until I was seventeen. I played hockey and ran long distances until my knees could handle no more. I rode a bicycle hundreds of miles a week until I had to replace my left hip with titanium. My body paid the price for my self-worth. Finally, physical exercise lost its ability to anesthetize the war in my mind.

How do you treat your body? Are you at war with your higher self? Is the battle manifesting itself in health problems?

The body will fail, and when it does, the creepy crawlers of our programming will make their way to the surface. Without exception, we must look at the issues that keep us from our true value as human beings. The light within us demands to be seen, and the diversion of athletics under the guise of high performance only serves to delay the enviable.

Of course we need to exercise and eat right, but not at the cost of broken body parts and wrecked internal organs.

There is a way out of the insanity. Lifting self-worth will right the ship. The bug in our brain can be patched and newer, healthier behaviors can be uploaded. Read the following affirmation for a stronger, healthier body image of yourself.

I am beautiful, flexible, and flowing.
My body is a magnificent example of health, power, and life.
I love my body; all parts work in harmony to serve my true purpose.
I love life and the vehicle God gave me.

Speak these words out loud every morning for at least ninety days. Look at yourself in the mirror and feel the gratitude of being loved.

You and I are worthy of a healthy body.

CHAPTER 49

FIND THE FIRE

Select only thoughts that contribute to the birth of your desires.

I spent a lot of time chasing the smoke instead of putting out the fire. I am distracted by the symptoms of my problems instead of facing the problem itself.

The road to higher self-worth is the process of identifying the fires that burn my success to the ground. I have a choice: let the fires rage uncontained or face them with the courage to stamp them out. It's not an easy choice, but one that must be made.

When I was young, I had the ability to bounce back from poor choices and the resolve to do better. As I got older, I lost the will to fight and turned to others for help.

I attended seminars, retreats, and workshops on a regular basis. Most times, I felt uplifted and empowered. I cleared the smoke one more time! However, the hot coals of my troubles still burned and eventually set fire to my success. Don't get me wrong, I love seminars, workshops, and retreats. They facilitate insights and feed my desire to learn more. But I can't rely on them for permanent change.

That's my job.

I grew up in a physically and verbally abusive home, and the language, emotions, and images imprinted in my Routine Engine carried well into my adult life. After I got sober, I spent a decade getting right with my family, making amends to those I harmed, and forgiving those who harmed me. Yet, my tattered self-image hid below the surface of my mind. There was always something deep within me that still burned. At a basic level, I never felt like I was good enough. I lacked the self-worth that I witnessed in others. I saw my friends and colleagues move faster than me, and I would punish myself for not having the motivation or confidence to take the next step in life.

Over time, I doubled my efforts, dug deeper, and found more burning coals. Still, I was confused as to why I could not get to the next level in my career or build the next great technology company. To make matters worse, I felt ungrateful for the life I built. By anyone's standards I'd done a good job with our kids and my career. But still, the coals burned and the smoke of self-loathing returned.

Through a lot of seeking and self-reflection, I discovered that lifting my worthiness changed how I felt about myself. When I practiced lifting my self-worth, permanent change took place. It was hard. At the time, I didn't have access to coaches who understood how to effectively build self-worth through language, meditation, and spiritual practices. The program described in this book is a strange brew of motivational psychology, neuroplasticity, and funky new age metaphysics. (Remember, I've tried everything!)

Combining these techniques with the assistance of a coach lifted my self-worth and accelerated my success—in any area I wished. It gave me the courage to look deeper and face the glaring defects of character that caused my poor behavior. Once found, I felt worthy of putting out the emotional fire and benefiting from the resulting peace. Higher self-worth enables me to look where I never wanted to look and dig where I never wanted to dig.

Focus on your core worthiness and watch the smoke clear from your life.

CHAPTER 5

IS THIS SERVING YOU?

You cannot draw from the outside what you need on the inside..

Over the years, I've built elaborate stories to justify my behavior. At one poin I wanted to be a professional poker player. I read many books, purchasec software that simulated game play, studied odds, and became a certified body language expert. Poker is a math game with the added dynamic of unpredictable human behavior.

I tracked my poker sessions and was completely transparent with my family a to where the money was going and how much I had won or lost. I even split my winnings with my wife, which ensured that she wouldn't give me crap should I pull ar all-nighter. Over the years, I won more than I lost. I was pretty good; however, I neve won a whole lot, either. I'd win two or three tournaments for $10,000 and then lose it later in the year. I'd have an up night followed by a down one. It's the nature of the game. Pros know this and so do I.

Then the strangest thing happened.

My friend Steve and I spent New Year's in Las Vegas. I played poker for thirty-six hours over a three-day period and only won one hundred dollars. Not what I call a killing. To make matters worse, I played the best poker of my life. I folded at the right times, made great calls, and bet heavy when I knew I could take the pot.

However, it didn't matter. Over the three days, the cards fell in crazy and bizarre ways. I'd carefully build my stack over several hours, only to have a crazy hand destroy it in less than a minute.

On the final night, I laid in bed, thinking about the prior days. Suddenly, a voice bellowed in my head, *Is this serving you?*

The voice was loud and authoritative. It was 2:00 a.m., and Steve was asleep in the next bed to me. The only sound in the room was the hum of the heater. The experience scared and rattled me.

Is what serving me? I thought. I lay on the bed, and thought about what had happened. I knew exactly what the voice was asking, and more importantly, from where it came. I spent three days playing poker and won a hundred dollars. That's three dollars an hour.

No, it was not serving me. I mentally answered.

On the drive home, I told Steve what had happened. He sat quietly for a minute. Steve is a measured friend and I knew he was thinking about what he was going to say.

"What are you going to do?" he said with the confidence tone of someone who knew exactly what I should do.

As we rolled across the California desert, I thought about my next move. Steve knew what had happened, and he was waiting for me to acknowledge the same truth. I finally replied, "I'm going to quit playing cards for a year and see what happens."

He smiled and said, "OK. That sounds good."

Over the year, I replaced my poker nights with spiritual seeking. I found a group of people who practice a Native American ceremony and hooked up with them. At the time, the world had dropped out from underneath me as if I had fallen into a deep sand trap with no footing to climb out. In hindsight, I was knocked off center by the voice in Las Vegas and its question "Is this serving you?" Was it the voice of God?

I didn't know. Or maybe, I didn't want to know.

It was a hard yet very important year. Over the months, confidence returned, and I started to feel better about myself.

A year later I returned to the poker tables. Feeling certain that I didn't have a gambling problem, I sat down with $300 and a stack of chips. Within an hour, I'd lost my buy-in and my edge. The money was gone and I rationalized an ATM visit.

Bad move.

By the end of the evening I was down $900 and feeling the stinging pain of regret. "Would have, could have, and should have" rang like the bells of Notre Dame. The damage to my ego, pride, and confidence rapidly lowered my self-worth. It was as if I turned the thermostat of worthiness down below freezing. It hurt like hell and offered a new and improved way to beat myself up.

I resolved to try again and regroup.

I returned to the poker tables a week later and managed a small win. OK, maybe I overreacted.

The following week—bang. Down $600—WTF?

The next week—a small win, and the next—a small loss.

Up and down, I repeated the cycle for another five months.

Is this serving you? rang in my head.

I remember the moment of clarity like it was this morning. I realized that I was gambling to beat myself up. Losing was far more valuable than winning. The money was the instrument of the abuser. Lose a little, small beating; lose a lot, bad beating.

It was clear: poker had been, and still was, my primary method of self-abuse.

I quit that day and have not gambled, in any form, since.

What is clear, and hopefully the lesson from this story, is that I was addicted to punishment. The pain of my poor behavior served a purpose; it kept away from my abundant life.

Our self-worth is a barrier, and it must be lifted to attain and keep our next success. Wealth, prosperity, love, health, connection, and strength can be yours. Self-worth can bar the beauty of life or open the doors of success.

Poker stole the energy from my soul. Each time I sat down, I tried to lie and steal money from another person. Under the guise of a game, I inflicted pain on others and myself. No one wins.

No, it didn't serve me.

I put down the cards several years ago and have not returned to the tables since. The need to punish myself is gone.

I am worthy of happiness. I am worthy of peace.

You are worthy of peace.

What's not serving you?

CHAPTER 51

WEAR THE SHOES THAT FIT

We've become numb to the pain of our existence.

I've worn a 10.5 shoe most of my life. No need to measure my feet, size ten and a half will do. Then, something odd happened. My massage therapist was working on my feet and said, "You need to wear larger shoes."

"Why?" I asked.

"Because your feet are twisted," she remarked. "Get your feet measured and buy some new shoes."

The next day I went to the shoe store and measured my feet. I was stunned to learn I had size 12 feet! I put on a pair of Ecco's (love that brand), and I felt like I was wearing scuba-diving flippers. I ignored my compulsive and habitual voice yelling, *You're a size 10.5*, and made the purchase. I tripped the first time I wore them and several times after that. However, after a few weeks, they felt pretty good. I swapped out my running shoes, and they felt great too! Soon, all the old shoes were out, and the new twelves were in.

On a trip to Boston, I wore an older pair of waterproof shoes—lots of snow and rain in Boston. They were 10.5 and hurt the whole trip. I couldn't wait to get them off. All I could think about was my massage therapist's advice to wear shoes that fit.

I spent thirty years with my feet in a knot, packed into shoes that didn't fit. Why? How did I not feel the pain of a pair of shoes almost two sizes too small?

Much like the emotional pain in my life, I'd become accustomed to it. Numb to the emotional discomfort of my self-worth, numb to the pain of injured body parts, numb to the pain of goals not achieved, and numb to the crushing stress of financial insecurity.

My feet were the physical manifestation of my life.

When I lifted my self-worth, I took off the tight shoes and allowed myself to feel the pleasure of shoes that fit. With each elevation of my self-worth, I allowed myself to feel the glorious emotion of confidence, purpose, and love.

You must be your biggest fan and learn to love every aspect of your body. Look at yourself in the mirror, and repeat the following statements:

You look amazing!
I'm ecstatic with how you look!
I love every part of you, and I know you love me.
I am a gift to the world, and I am a gift to me.

Read and practice The Gift. It's specifically designed to lift your physical well-being. The readings are meant to free you of the mental torture of "I don't like my body."

I love my body now. It has taken some time to change the language of loathing to the language of love. I did it and so can you.

It's OK to feel good.

CHAPTER 52

PURPOSE IS THE TENT POLE OF LIFE

Purpose rises from an inner source and has a nameless voice.

Purpose enables one to endure anything. Friedrich Nietzsche said, "*He who has a why to live can bear almost any how.*" Purpose causes us to rise to the task, fuels confidence, and gets us out of bed without struggle.

Purpose is the tent pole of life.

You are worthy of a purpose and worthy of attaining it. The size of your tent is determined by the size of your purpose and the worthiness to hold up the tent. Some trive for huge tents while others enjoy the comfort of a smaller one. When you have a purpose, the magic of life surrounds you.

There are numerous influential people in my life; they've inspired me to take action and go beyond my limits. In my youth, they were baseball coaches and math teachers. As an adult, they're men and women with happy lives and giving souls. They believe in me, inspire me, and encourage me to chase my goals and to accept them when they arrive. My mentors act with purpose—the purpose to help and encourage me.

If you don't know your purpose, be willing to look for it. Start where you are and make a decision to seek an answer. Too often I speak to people who want to know their purpose, yet make no effort to seek the answer. At a deep level, they don't want to know their purpose because it would force them to take action. When you know your purpose, you must act accordingly. People who live their purpose are living their highest desire—the highest level of worthiness.

The size of your tent is defined by the size of your purpose.
Know why you're here and what you're to do; then go do it.
You are worthy of living your purpose.

CHAPTER 53

WE SEE WHAT WE ARE

The evidence of your worthiness surrounds you.

I love dogs. Our family has a rescue dog named Boone. He's a German Shepherd mutt with floppy ears and a calm demeanor. At dawn I take Boone to the local park where he finds the scents of other animals irresistible. Most days I'm the only one around as we calmly move from tree to tree. On occasion we encounter other dogs roaming free, off leash, and I get mad when they come up on us uncontrolled. When Boone was five years old, another Shepherd attacked him while my wife was on a walk. The thought of this occurring again causes me significant grief.

A strange coincidence happened every time I engaged a dog off leash. I noticed most were Boxers. As a breed, Boxers are typically mellow and make good family pets, yet the ones I encountered were far from mellow.

Why was I constantly running into Boxers off their leash? What is it in me that attracts aggressive and uncontrolled Boxers?

The answer was not hard to find.

When I was five years old, I stepped on the family dog and he mauled me. His name was Rowdy, and he was a Boxer. I still have the scar above my eye and the deep fear of uncontrolled canines. To this day, I freeze at the sight of a large dog. The bug in my Routine Engine is what attracts large angry Boxers. I fear dogs off leash, specifically Boxers, and I attract them when I walk Boone.

This is the power of the subconscious mind and the belief system it holds. The events in my life are the manifestation of my subconscious routines and images from emotional events. Until I'm able to free myself of the mauling and the story around it, I'll continue to attract dogs that threaten Boone and me.

We must address the pain and hurt that exist and make a decision to change how we see ourselves relative to the pain. I must change the dog attack story and see myself as worthy of safety and protection, as a friend to all dogs.

Accepting that you're partially, or in whole, the source of your pain is difficult. If you don't like the people around you, listen to them because they reflect how you feel about yourself. When I speak fewer words, there's room for others to reflect who I am. It's like having a mirror to my subconscious and the inner workings of my soul.

Step back and consider the challenging people in your life. They're telling you what needs to change in you. Worthy people go deep to find the bugs in their brains. Friends, family, neighbors, and colleagues reflect the bugs.

When you change the bug, the reflection will change as well.

PART 3

THE PRACTICE OF
BUILDING SELF-WORTH

CHAPTER 54

THE KEY

If you're not grateful for what you have, you certainly will not be grateful for what you'll get.

The human brain is a muscle that can be exercised, conditioned, and improved. We can change our thinking and our experiences for the better by changing our programming. The following exercises will bring dramatic change. The foundation of this work was drawn from thirty years of experience working with men and women who started at the lowest possible point of self-worth and have grown into amazing successes. If it worked for them, it will certainly work for you.

It starts with changing the language in your brain. Call it brainwashing if you like, but from where I stand, my brain needed a good scrubbing. We'll find and celebrate small wins, build on them, and launch to even bigger wins. Very quickly, we'll see change. We'll feel better, act better, and smile more. A sense of relief will roll over us like a cool summer breeze. We will see the path home and run to its comfort.

CHAPTER 5

START WHERE YOU ARE

All doors need to be open.

At its core, self-worth sets the tone for all my experiences. Like a faucet, it controls the flow of positive and negative emotions and defines the quality of my life. The higher my self-worth—expressed as self-love and self-esteem—the happier and more successful I am. When my subconscious mind believes I'm good and worthy of good things, I naturally do positive, self-esteem-building actions. More importantly, I allow abundance, love, peace, wealth, and success to flow into my life because I'm worthy to receive it.

Building self-worth has a compounding effect. The more I improve how I feel about myself, the more good I allow to flow. It's an endless source of abundance and love with no limits because self-worth has no limits.

The first step is to determine your level of worthiness. Do the following test of your self-worth.

Step 1—Go to the bathroom and close the door. Make sure the space is private and you will not be disturbed.

Step 2—Face the mirror. Look yourself in the eyes and say "You are whole, perfect, strong, powerful, loving, harmonious, and happy. You are beautiful, smart, and a winner. You are an awesome person, and I love you."

Step 3—Be honest. Do you believe what you say?

Listen to your emotions. What are they telling you? If you feel uneasy, frightened, shameful, embarrassed, dishonest, or scared, you may want to consider the solutions in this book. These emotions are common for those starting out on this path.

CHAPTER 56

PRACTICE 1: TURN OFF THE BAD NEWS

First, stop consuming the bad news or watching any program that doesn't lift your emotions in a positive direction. Do the following:

1. *Turn off and avoid all bad news programs including blogs, television, radio, videos, and podcasts.*
2. *Stop receiving news feeds in your e-mail.*
3. *Unsubscribe to news alerts.*
4. *Block social-media friends that post negative crap. We all know who they are; cut them out.*
5. *Unsubscribe from social-media feeds that don't support a positive experience.*

This fire hose of negative emotion does not serve you. It floods your mind with images and language that form the basis of your behaviors. Protect the portals of you mind.

CHAPTER 57

PRACTICE 2: THE "I'M SORRY" INFECTION

The phrase "I'm sorry" is killing your career and relationships. Yep, these two words are termites in your foundation and eat away at your success. "I'm sorry" has a huge negative affect on your self-worth. Think about it, why are you even saying "I'm sorry"? We say "I'm sorry" because we don't want to offend anyone. We're so worried about other people's opinions that we are constantly apologizing for natural human behavior.

One of the biggest infections is e-mail. Consider this example:

"Hi, Bill, sorry I didn't get back to you sooner but...(fill in the blame phrase here)."

We use "I'm sorry" in our everyday business language or navigating a crowd. Next time you're in a coffee shop, notice the barrage of "I'm sorrys" dropped by people trying to order a latte.

We're not sorry! Use words that express what you mean, such as "Excuse me" or "Do you mind?" Saying "I'm sorry" tells the other person "I'm not worth anything. I'm in the way, and I hope I didn't offend you."

Here's your assignment: only say "I'm sorry" when you need to apologize for your behavior. The times when you'll need to say "I'm sorry" are clear. Then, when you do say "I'm sorry," the words have meaning.

The results of eliminating "I'm sorry" from your vocabulary will blow your mind. Your colleagues and friends will change how they treat you. Your e-mails will lack the

stupid excuses that no one believes anyways. If your e-mail is late, it doesn't require reason as to why you're late. Just respond.

Consider the two contrasting examples below:

1. Hi, Bill, sorry that I didn't get back to you sooner. The week was crazy busy. Here are the reports you requested. Again, sorry for the delay.
2. Hi, Bill, here are the reports you requested. Let me know if there is anything else you need.

Believe me, response #2 is enough, and it doesn't lower your self-worth. You may be thinking *But response #1 sounds better.* That's because you have a worthiness issue.

We are human and say and do things that keep us from our true potential. "I'm sorry" literally means I am the emotion of regret. People who are working to elevate their self-worth only apologize when an apology is needed. They're mindful of the words they speak and know the power they embody.

Only say "I'm sorry" when you really mean it.

Start today.

CHAPTER 58

PRACTICE 3: PUT ON YOUR OXYGEN MASK

Before an airplane takes off, the flight attendants demonstrate how to use the oxygen mask and instruct you to put your mask before helping others. You can't help others until you help yourself first.

Many people ignore their needs. They sacrifice their family, career, health, and financial well-being under the guise of selflessness. However, this has the opposite effect. We must take care of ourselves before we can take care of another. Here's a list of self-care actions you can implement:

- Vacation—Americans wasted a record 650 million vacation days in 2016. This staggering statistic is hard evidence that we do not value our personal time away from our job. If you have a job that provides vacation time, take all of it and disconnect while on vacation. No checking e-mail or answering messages while away. It is a critical self-worth building action you can do.
- Weekends—If you work Monday through Friday, take both Saturday and Sunday away from the e-mail and phone. Disconnect. If you work the weekend, be sure to disconnect on your days off.
- Maintenance light is on in your car. Get it serviced.
- Wear good shoes that fit your feet.
- Celebrate your wins (this is a big miss for most).
- Be present for your children. Turn off the mobile and e-mail.
- Get a massage. Let someone else heal your aches.
- Hug your father or mother.

- Say yes when someone offers to buy you lunch.
- Allow someone to throw you a party, such as a birthday.
- Tell your wife or husband how happy you are being married to them.
- Take a walk on the beach, in a park, or in the mountains. Get outside and feel the sun on your face

Massage

I started the process of self-care with massage. I signed up for a monthly service—one hour per month. The first few times were difficult, as I didn't like to be touched. Eventually I came to like massage and increased the sessions to twice a month. I found a great therapist, and she worked on me in a way that I never knew possible. Apparently, the body holds trauma in the muscles, and my neck and back were holding on to a lot.

One particular session she was working my shoulders and I completely lost emotional control. I cried and howled for ten minutes as an avalanche of emotion burst out of me. Never before had I felt such a release of emotion: it was primitive, deep in my bones, and the energy that came out was so intense that I felt it would never stop. She simply kept working on me and let me be as it passed.

Over the months, this occurred three more times. I value massages, hugs, and human touch as never before. It is self-love and self-worth, and I gladly accept it.

You must find ways to take care of yourself. Celebrate the wins. Go to the beach or swim in a lake; hike in the mountains or play in a park.

You're worthy of love. Ask for it and allow it to be given.

Start your journey. Choose one self-care act from the above list and enjoy the ride.

CHAPTER 59

PRACTICE 4: LISTEN

Listening is a powerful tool. Energy flows between the speaker and the listener. When you're present for a conversation, you are more connected to the speaker. As you develop your self-worth, the practice of listening becomes your most powerful success tool.

Listening helps you understand how you're thinking. By listening to others, you gain a deeper knowledge of your own voice—the one that rattles in the background while the speaker is talking.

Listeners are always welcome everywhere. If you're a sales person, listening will close more deals than talking or even asking for the order.

I coached an insurance salesman to simply listen and get to know his clients. "Don't focus on closing the business," I told him. "Try to learn as much as you can about what makes the client who they are, and then wait for them to ask you for the order." Within a month, his clients would regularly say "So how do we start?" He works 50 percent less and makes twice as much as he did before. No joke. Half the work, double the money.

People want to be heard. In business, the skill of listening is so rarely used that it almost seems unfair as a sales tactic.

Listening is a characteristic of a worthy individual. They don't need to interrupt, talk over, grandstand, or even give an opinion. They smile, laugh, and are secure in their skin no matter what is going on or who has the spotlight. They wait to be asked for their opinion. When they speak, people listen.

Here are the key areas that improve as you develop your listening skills:

- **Your Inner Voice**—The practice of listening to your inner voice is so critical for your success that it's importance cannot be overstated. You need to know what you're thinking, and the way to know what you're thinking is to be aware of your inner voice. The Routine Engine is always running, and we must learn to catch the thoughts that prevent us from listening to others. Listening to your inner voice and changing its direction (to a positive one) is the muscle you need to discover and exercise. Meditation is a practice that allows you to witness your thoughts and train your mind to be calm. I've included a section on meditation that will help you develop this valuable skill yourself.

- **Our Children**—Children know when you're not present. Their ability to sense "nonpresence" is an instinct they're born with and is always on display. "Daddy, look at me" were my children's most common words. Children know when their parents are not emotionally connected to them. It's as if they have radar, constantly scanning the area for those who are watching, good or bad. Listening and being present for our children builds their self-worth. Building a child's self-worth is amazingly rewarding and critical to their development. Listening is absolutely critical; never miss the opportunity.

- **In Business**—Listening in business engagements is the most overlooked skill of all. Forget the MBA; develop your listening skills. Fine-tune your listening and know when to speak. At the time of this writing, I lead a cloud consulting practice. We help large clients move their data centers (over one thousand servers) to the public cloud. The work is amazing and very complex. In most situations, our clients are scared of the change that cloud brings to their world. They don't understand what needs to be done; that's why they hire us. They need someone they can trust—really trust. Careers are on the line, and as consultants, our ability to listen to our clients vent their frustrations, fears, and worries is critical. Typically I ask one question: "What are your plans for the cloud?" and then sit back and listen. Occasionally they want feedback or ask a couple questions about how we do our migration services, but on the whole, they talk and tell us what they need. Finally, they ask the most important question: "How do we get started?" Totally amazing! However, you have to have control of your inner voice. So often I see sales people preparing their response before the client finishes speaking. The client may not consciously sense that the sales person has disconnected, but they subconsciously know it. What I have found is this: clients buy from people they like. Everyone loves a good listener. Always. It never fails. Turn off your response and increase your income.

- **Friends and Family**—"Robert is always there for me" are the words I hear the most. I listen to my friends and family. Listening is my expression of love. "Let's meet and have a cup of coffee" are my favorite words. I feel complete when someone unloads a burden, and takes a breath. Usually I say "What's going on?" and listen. The road to real happiness is through quieting your inner voice. When you turn down the volume, good things happen for you and those around you. The higher your self-worth, the more your family and friends want to be around you. By listening to them, you lift their worthiness.
- **On the Telephone**—People know when you're checked out on the phone. Whether on a conference call or speaking with your partner, the person on the other side of the line knows you've mentally checked out. The energy is immediately lost when you turn your attention to e-mail or materials on your desk. The person or people on the call may not know it consciously, but they definitely know it subconsciously because your energy is disconnected from them. Stay present in all aspects of your communications. Your success—financially and personally—depends upon it.

istening becomes easier as you elevate your self-worth and calm the negative voices n your brain's Routine Engine. Those with higher self-worth know that we're all con-ected and there's a bond of energy that binds us together. Listening acknowledges hat energy; it amplifies and communicates to the speaker how we care.

Listening is the act of loving yourself. Love is a powerful emotion and moves peo-le to act.

Shut Up and Listen Exercise

've employed numerous listening techniques throughout my career but none more eneficial than the "shut up and listen" technique. If you're preparing your response

before the speaker has finished, then you're not listening. One interesting by-product of listening is that people believe you agree with their position. I've neatly avoided numerous conflicts related to religion, politics, taking sides in divorces, and a whole host of potential problems because I simply listened to the person. Very rarely do they ask for your opinion. The reason is straightforward: people don't want to know your opinion; they want you to listen to them.

Here's the practice: when you're listening, say and do nothing, simply stand still and look at the speaker. Forget the "active listening" techniques taught by communication coaches where you respond and acknowledge the speaker; it interrupts the flow of communication. Listen and wait until it's your time to speak.

The Speech

I recall a speech I gave to several hundred business professionals on listening.

We were in a large ballroom, late morning, and I was the third speaker in a long day of sessions. I had thirty minutes to illustrate my point, so I decided drive home the lesson with the power of this exercise.

I asked the audience to stand and pair off. As they stood and selected their partner, I instructed them to pick the speaker and listener for the exercise. Once settled, proposed the following question:

"For the speaker, your topic is this - What would you change about the world?"

I let the depth and weight of the question navigate its way through their consciousness. After several moments I said, "You have 3 minutes to tell your partner what you would change about the world."

I continued, not waiting for the audience to start chatting. "Now, listeners. You are to stand still and listen to the speaker, without moving, responding, or nodding."

A wave of uneasiness rolled through the crowd. After I settled them down, I said "Go!"

The room exploded with solutions to the world's most pressing problems. The ballroom was alive with excitement while the listeners stood perfectly still. The bridled tension of the listeners overtook the room; they deeply want to respond, to disagree, to add their opinion, to jump into the mix!

Yet, they were locked, silent, and motionless.

For them, the three minutes was an eternity.

Mercifully, I call, "Time!"

The room burst into laughter and relief.

"Now, swap roles," I continue. "Speakers, what would you change about the world? You have three minutes, go!"

Predictably, the room launched into indecipherable chatter and emotion.

I stood in the center of the room, watching. Some of the listeners could not follow the rules, they simply lacked the ability to stand still or not respond. There were a few, however, that absolutely got the point of the exercise. Motionless, they held the space for the speaker to go deep with their conviction, their belief, and their passion for what should change in our world today. The moment was not lost on the speaker and the listener.

"Time!" I say.

Predictably, a wave of relief washed over the audience. I asked them to have a seat.

"What was that like?" I asked.

A tall man stood and said, "Very uncomfortable. It was difficult to do nothing."

"I couldn't do it", said a woman in the back.

I asked, "Who was in control of the conversation?"

Silence. Then, a hand appeared. "The listener," a young woman in her twenties said.

"Why?"

"Because the less I responded, the more the speaker knew I was listening to what he had to say."

"Why did that matter?" I pushed.

Again, silence. Finally she said, "I was totally there for her and she trusted me to hear what she had to say. It was a safe space."

"Yes!" I congratulated her. "The listener creates the space for the speaker to be heard, and being heard is the highest form of love you can give to another."

The audience sat quiet as I walked between the tables. I said nothing, letting the speaker-listener role swap. They were in control of me and had always been.

The "shut up and listen" technique is amazingly powerful. In business, the speaker will tell you all you'll need to know regarding the transaction - if you keep quiet. If they want to know more, they'll stop and ask. In personal relationships, the "shut up and

listen" technique can repair shattered marriages, right problem children, and save u from permanent mother-in-law damage.

When I sit quietly, with no agenda, I see myself reflected in the language of th speaker. They speak what I feel. It's a great reflection of the language, emotions, an images within my Routine Engine. If I don't like what is being said, I have the opportu nity to look within me and see what it is I don't like.

Practice listening. It will change your life—all for the better.

CHAPTER 60

PRACTICE 5: MEDITATION

When I started the practice of meditation, I was able to get a few days in, maybe even a week, and then I'd fall off the practice. At one point, I amassed a couple weeks of consistent meditation, with each session lasting upward of twenty minutes. However, I could never keep it up. Fixing my resolve, I'd go to a retreat and commit to improving my practice. I'm good at the forty-yard dash, but I could never run the marathon.

I knew the development of a consistent meditation practice was important. Every book I read about self-improvement and the attainment of a degree of happiness suggested meditation. I wanted to slow down my thinking and train my thoughts. I considered it a high priority but had little success. It was really frustrating and it fed my limited self-worth language.

"I can't meditate" is the repeated mantra of self-deprecation and suggests that I am broken and flawed.

When I did meditate, I received the benefits and physically felt better. I was calmer, in control of my emotions, and had a sense of peace. What I know now is that I was getting closer to God and was able to touch the transcendent in a way that I never thought possible. I really enjoyed it.

Yet, every time I got momentum and felt the benefits, I'd quit.

I asked myself, "Why do I quit?"

Why do I avoid meditating when it pays such high dividends? The rationalization, the resistance, and the justification seemed to be in every cell of my body, telling me, "You can let meditation slide." I lacked the muscle to keep going. This was another character flaw I held up as evidence that I sucked. The peaceful life was meant for someone else, not me.

I was battling low self-worth, and until I was able to install new language in my head, I'd be stuck repeating the mantras of personal disgust. As long as the benefits of meditation continued, my Routine Engine would push back and deny those benefits through procrastination, justification, and avoidance.

This is the key message of this book: self-worth is buried in the subconscious and is exposed through poor behavior and the avoidance of actions that are good for us. To me, there is no other answer. People with higher self-worth simply do things that support the betterment of their situation—health, relationships, spirit, and finances. Limited self-worth people avoid positive, character-building actions, whether they intend to or not.

In the end, I had to lift my self-worth to a point where I could gain control. This happened when the language in my Routine Engine went from, *You are not good*, to, *I am worthy of love and peace. I am love and peace.*

Do the readings in the back of this book and change the language of your subconscious. From there, you'll gain the power to start meditating and receive the benefits it has to offer.

The Act of Meditating

There are numerous forms of meditation, each with their own particular stated benefits and purposes. I've outlined the basics in this chapter for the purposes of a starter. You'll need to take the action and deepen your practice by means that align with your beliefs, customs, and intentions.

My experience with meditation started with a weekly group that met on Thursday mornings. Each week, a volunteer would lead the session. This gave the leader a chance to learn a practice and teach the practice to the group. From this foundation, I learned how to meditate and bring the practice into my life.

The following is a primer to get you started meditating. It is intended to help demystify the practice and remove the cultural or religious overtones that tend to keep people away from the practice.

1. **Showing Up**—The number one requirement of meditation is the attempt to meditate. Showing up is the first rule of meditation. Making a commitment

to meditate every day is critical; even if it's to do one minute in the morning, we must do one minute every day. Remember, routine and repetition are your friends. Therefore, your brain's Routine Engine will come to expect the peace of meditation every day. Once the subconscious mind is addicted to its daily break, you'll parlay the winnings into all areas of your life. Therefore, showing up is the most important part of meditation.

2. **Location**—Find a safe, quiet spot indoors where you will not be interrupted. For me, it is my office at home. I started in the bathroom, on the closed toilet seat. Yes, I know, not very elegant but it served the purpose and got me uninterrupted time to start the practice. I know many people who use the driver's seat of their car. It's quiet, safe and protected. Regarding meditating outdoors, I do not suggest starting the practice outside.

   a. You want the emotional security of safety. Sitting quietly, with your eyes closed, in outdoors, initially does not bring about the desired effect. Also, insects tend to interrupt the flow. Start indoors, and after you have a solid discipline, you can venture into the great outdoors.

3. **Readings**—Before I meditate, I read my Success Statement. My Success Statement is a short statement of my goals—financial, spiritual, physical, mental, and personal including relationships. Occasionally, I switch up the readings with affirmations with an understanding of what I am doing. I impress into my subconscious mind my desires. The impression period is usually ninety days; however, I've found it takes less time when you've cleared your mind of broken thinking. Pick readings that matter to you. There are a number of them in The Gift section of this book. Start with that section for ninety days. Once you have acquired the discipline, you can branch to others.

4. **Music**—My preference is to meditate without music. A friend of mine mentioned that our brain gets addicted to the music and requires it to get into a meditative state. That made sense to me. I want to identify my thinking anywhere, under any circumstances, and music seems to be more of a distraction than help. However, I know many meditators who like and leverage music with great benefit. Find what works for you.

5. **Guided**—I will, from time to time, follow a guided meditation in an effort to discover a block, but once discovered, I typically go back to silent meditation

with a timer. Done well, guided meditations are amazing and open doors that may appear to be shut. I've used guided meditations to help me understand my purpose and to clear my foggy vision. There are many paths to the mountaintop; find what works for you.

6. **Time and Duration**—I meditate once a day for twenty minutes. Most meditation practices suggest a twenty-minute session upon awakening. I've adopted this practice, and it seems to be a perfect mix for me. I get up at 5:00 a.m. every day, go to the bathroom, do what I need to do, and head to my office. There, I do my readings, meditate, and say a few prayers to center me. Once complete, about thirty minutes, I'm good to go and ready for the world.

7. **Breathing**—Most practices teach some form of breathing technique whereby you focus on the breath moving in and out of your body. Witnessing your breath, moving in and out, has the effect of clearing your thoughts and moving you into the present moment. This simple technique is the foundation of my meditation practice and brings me back to the present whenever mentally wander off. Try this technique. Imagine your mind is a puppy. Your goal is to train the puppy to stay. You move the puppy in front of you, release it, and wait. As expected, the puppy wanders off for no apparent reason; simple curiosity gets the best of her. You move the puppy back and do it again. With each return, the puppy slowly learns that it must stay in front of you. Hopefully you do this with love and kindness. Your mind works the same way. Simply return to the breath and the present moment. You'll train your mind to stay and not become a victim of random thinking.

8. **Posture**—I learned to meditate sitting on the edge of a chair or stool. I roll my hips forward to straighten my spine and lay my hands palms down on my knees. Palms up or palms down, whatever feels natural to you. There are other meditation practices that encourage lying down or sitting comfortably in a chair. I don't have an opinion on any of those—just that you're consistent with the meditation practice. For me, posture helps me maintain my focus on the breath. Again, find what works for you.

9. **Clothing**—I meditate in my daily clothes; however, I loosen my belt and unbutton my pants to free my waist. Loosening my pants helps my breathing by freeing my stomach to move in and out with my breath; it's also comfortable

10. **Apps**—I highly recommend using a mobile phone app. I use *Insight Timer* for the Android and iPhone. It offers useful tools for both guided and timed meditations, as well as useful features for connecting with other meditators.
11. **Coming Out**—Once my meditation has concluded, I slowly open my eyes and stretch my body by standing up and raising my arms over my head. I bring myself to the current moment and say a set of prayers that have become my daily practice.

I hope these suggestions help your meditation practice. Once you develop the routine, you will surely branch out and find more techniques that help you improve your practice. I have, and I know you will too.

Taylor's Story

My wife and I read to our two children regularly, and when they were little, we read the same books several hundred times! One day, Taylor wanted me to read *Good Night Moon* for the fiftieth time, and I obliged. We sat on the floor, and I started from memory. My mind drifted elsewhere, dealing with some problem my inner voice felt was a higher priority than being present with my son. I was mindlessly reading the first few pages when I felt his little hand on my cheek. He stood in front of me, staring into my eyes. He pulled my face to the book, sat back down, and waited for me to continue. To this day, I feel the heat of his hand on my cheek. The experience was so profound, and I will never forget it. My three-year-old son knew more about presence and listening than I did. He knew I wasn't there, put his hand on my face, turned my head, and demanded my attention; he required my emotion, energy, and love.

He didn't want me to read the book; he wanted my love through the act of reading the book. Reading the book was the tool he used to get love, presence; he wanted his self-worth lifted.

To this day, he's such a gentleman—purposeful and gentle.

CHAPTER 6

EXERCISE 6 MOVEMENT AND DIET

Moving your body is critical to your ability to attain and retain success. In his wonderful book, *Brain Rules*, John J. Medina details twelve brain rules to help the average Joe increase productivity, intelligence, and well-being. Medina's first rule is exercise, and he details the brain benefits from an active life style. They include dramatically lower rates of brain-related diseases and issues as we age. His data show considerable evidence that movement—walking, aerobic exercise, strength training—two to three times a week consistently lifts brain productivity. We simply have better brain function when we move.

I couldn't agree more. Exercise is critical to those who want to feel better, not only for gaining higher brain productivity but also for reinforcing the love one has for his or her body. Exercise and proper diet are the main contributors to a healthy body and are often the difference between aging gracefully and sliding into mental oblivion.

Higher self-worth is reflected in a healthy body. This can be more difficult than other self-worth aspects of your personality. Everybody reacts differently to the things we ingest. Since every brain is unique, the reactions to sugar, coffee, cocaine, alcohol, McDonald's, hotdogs, and marijuana are different from person to person.

Change Your Thinking and Get Moving

Movement increases blood flow, which increases the number of veins in your brain (as well as in the other parts of your body). When the brain receives more nutrients, it functions better and communicates to The Creator more effectively.

By lifting your love for your body, you'll naturally eat better and exercise more. Higher self-worth wants a better body, and naturally acts to attain it.

My Attractive, Perfectly Healthy Body

Read this affirmation every day for ninety days. The language, emotions, and images of good health, mindful eating, and love for your body will take hold. You'll naturally stop fighting exercise programs and bad food and freely want to take walks and feel the movement of your body.

I am an attractive health-conscious human being.
I have a healthy image of myself with increasing energy, vitality, and grace.
I am vibrant and alive.
I believe my health is the greatest of human blessings.
I desire healthy food.
I am happy and grateful that I exercise every day.
Every day in every way, I'm getting better and better.
I am flexible and flowing.
My body knows what to do with food, and I trust it.
Every cell in my body is loved and healthy.
I love my body. Every part is perfectly fitted to me, as God would have it be.
I see the beauty in all people.
I am grateful for all the things my body allows me to do.
I nourish my body with healthy foods, rest, and exercise.
I enjoy my body.
I am perfect and complete.
I take care of my body, inside and out.
I eat mindfully.
I love my body for taking care of me.
Thank you for my body.

THE GIFT

INTRODUCTION

The Gift is a set of readings that focuses on lifting self-worth. It replaces the bugs in our brain with language that supports an improved life. In a short period of time, the new language takes root and naturally changes the programming of your Routine Engine. The Gift is a collection of readings—each with a specific purpose. These words completely changed my life and the lives of many, many women and men.

Here are the instructions for the readings:

#1—Read all readings every day in a quiet private place. Safety is important. Most people feel embarrassed when they start. Don't fight the embarrassment; just find a place that is quiet and emotionally safe. The bathroom works well. The inside of a parked car is also a good spot, especially if you forget to do the readings in the morning.

#2—Read out loud. Reading out loud helps to keep you focused. I have found myself reading to myself and not remember what I read. Reading out loud works.

#3—Read with a smile and emotion. Put emotion into the readings. The more emotion invested, the better and faster the process. Emotion helps the brain absorb the information. Think about 9/11. Just about everyone knows where he or she was at that time. Emotion drives memories and brain changes. Put emotion into the Readings.

#4—Read in the morning, before you get going, and at night, before bed. This is the discipline. We must prepare our day and emphasize our value before we close our eyes.

#5—Read while looking into a mirror. This is where people feel the most uncomfortable. Mirror work is also the highest payback. If you're not able to look at

yourself in the mirror, the exercises still work; however, experience suggests that those who are able to do the readings in the mirror experience results faster. It's important to give yourself a break. Work your way to the mirror when you can. *#6—Read for at least ninety days in a row.* Consistency is the *most* important action. Daily routine is what changes the brain. Think about riding a bicycle. At first, it's very complex when you're highly focused on learning the routine. Then there comes a point where your Routine Engine takes over and you no longer need to focus as hard. You're aware but not lost in concentration. The readings, when read daily for ninety days, enforce the language of higher self-worth. We are using our brain's compulsive behavior to our benefit and reprogramming The Routine Engine. Teach the brain the routine of higher self-worth and we change our world!

Only you can do the readings. Ownership of your success is as simple as making a decision to improve your self-worth. The universe of infinite intelligence will do the rest!

Reading #1—The Gift

I am a gift. Everywhere I go, people are happy to see me. They smile and encourage me at every step. Supporters and believers surround me.

I am beautiful. Every part of my body is perfectly shaped and a gift to me. I see beauty in everyone and love every part of my body.

I am awesome. I serve others because I like to help, and I receive incredible joy from their happiness. I love my fellow man in every way, and they love me.

I am smart. I know that I can achieve anything I want and am willing to change my actions to achieve my goals. I see opportunity everywhere.

I am a receiver. I'm open and willing to receive the abundance of the universe now. I'm wealthy in every way.

I am forgiven. I'm forgiven for all the actions that I believe hurt others, and I forgive everyone who I believe harmed me.

I am a gift and am worthy of love.

Reading #2—I Believe

I believe in the power of my thoughts. I know what I am doing and understand how to change my life.
I believe God always says yes.
I believe divine love shines from within me.
I believe self-worth controls my experiences.
I believe all is possible through higher self-worth.
I believe in prayer and understand how prayer works.
I believe money is how God flows material abundance to me.
I believe God sends me exactly what I believe I am worth.
I believe I am love, peace, light, and beauty.
I believe in compassion and speak highly of all people.
I believe I am a beautiful example of success.
I believe my welfare comes first and I act accordingly.
I believe I am of maximum service to those who need me.
I believe I shape my world and experience what I want.
I believe I am the creator of my world.
I believe there is only one source and it listens to me.
I believe in myself—always.

Reading #3—My True Definite Purpose in Life

I follow my highest desire and take action toward its realization.
I am true to myself and all men and women. I commit to treat them as I wish to be treated.

I always seek positive outcomes for all parties involved in business transactions and personal relationships.

I elevate my self-worth for the attainment of my true purpose in life.

I allow others to help me because of my willingness to help them.

I love all people, of all shapes, sizes, colors, and creeds.

I am one with all people and they are one with me.

I make great decisions and feel a deep sense of peace knowing my choices are always perfect.

I am the best I have ever been and know I will be even better tomorrow.

I am a winner—now and forever.

My success is preordained because I am the *best* at what I do.

I love my life and all those in it.

The road to my true purpose is beautiful, glorious, and brilliant.

Reading #4—My Abundance

I open myself to all the wealth of the universe. I allow financial, personal, physical and spiritual prosperity to flow into my life. I open myself to the infinite intelligence of all ages and trust that it has my highest benefit at heart. I allow abundance to freely flow money, wealth, and prosperity into my life. It is done.

Reading #5—Advancement and Decisions

I always make the right decisions. Every decision I make is perfect and is exactly the right choice at the right time. If a different decision is to be made, God will send me more information, and I will make a different decision. I always make the perfect decision—every time.

Reading #6—I Love Our Clients

I love our clients.

They are the best clients any company could have. They help us improve our products and services, and give us praise when we do a good job.

My clients are the best clients any person could have. They genuinely want to do business with me and want to help me wherever they can.

Today, I will do my best to meet our clients' expectations of our products and services. I am committed to serving them to my fullest ability.

I love our clients because they love to laugh with us.

I love our clients because they teach us something new every day.

I love our clients because I can talk to them for hours about my work. It makes my job enjoyable, and that is an *awesome* feeling!

I love our clients because they take the time and effort to give good feedback that improves our products and services.

We charge a fair price for our services and our clients are happy to pay it.

I love our clients.

Reading #7—Lucky Person

I am the lucky person.

Good fortune follows me and rewards my good deeds.

Everywhere I look, people are good-hearted and want to help me achieve good things.

Money and prosperity flow to me with ease with a genuine desire to please me.

I see life as a joy that brings me the rewards of a positive attitude, or as others see it—luck.

Everybody who believes they are lucky is lucky. Every opportunity in front of me is brought to me because I imagined it, thought it, and therefore my luck is exactly to the proportion I believe it to be.

I am the luckiest person in the world. Endless good fortune comes my way. And I gladly accept it.

Mantras

The first mantra is from *The Big Leap* by Gay Hendricks. Hendricks believes this mantra will keep you focused while you are out and about. I agree; it has worked for me. Repeating this mantra throughout the day helps bring me back to the present moment and enforces my desire for higher self-worth.

> *"I expand in abundance, success, and love every day as I lead, motivate, and inspire others to do the same."*

The second mantra is from the book *The Master Key System* by Charles F. Haanel. The affirmation incorporates every single thing any human being can want and that this affirmation will bring about harmonious conditions to all things. I agree. I love this mantra as it grounds me and helps me deal with my sometimes hectic life.

> *"I am whole, perfect, strong, powerful, loving, harmonious and happy."*

CHAPTER 63

FINAL THOUGHTS

I hope you have found what I have found: a solution that works under any condition or circumstance. Self-worth is the heart of the matter. It controls confidence and motivation, initiates action, and is at the core of desire. Self-worth is the father of our well-being and the saboteur of our success. It is a sword that swings both ways, and we must know how to wield it to our benefit.

The ladder of progress is never-ending. There is always another mountain to climb, whether it is financial, physical, personal, or spiritual. We're an expanding life force, always creating and becoming, moving from form to form, evolving.

Worthiness is your passport to progress. As you rise in worthiness, you'll notice how much you love people. You'll want to see them succeed and teach them what you've learned. It is the natural progress of becoming.

Take what you've learned and tell others about it. However, you cannot give away what you do not have. Become a witness of change; lift your deserving and God will meet it beyond measure. Give away The Gift to those who are listening, who see your progress, and who want to know how you have changed your life.

Your success will amplify through those you touch.

May you walk in the light.

ABOUT THE AUTHOR

Robert Christiansen is an executive, entrepreneur, mentor, public speaker and master coach. Robert sits on the fifty-yard line and is witness to the critical technology changes impacting the way we do business across the globe. With great change comes great fear, and Robert is passionate about ensuring that self-worth is elevated in our professional and personal lives so we can move past our fears and be ready to accept and take advantage of the incredible inventions and improvements headed our way.

Robert is the president of Motive For Life, a professional coaching, event, and publishing company based in Lake Forest, California. Robert's thirty years of work in the field of alcohol and drug addiction led him to his discovery of the relationship between self-worth and sabotage behaviors that affect millions of people around the world. Motive For Life is dedicated to bringing this solution to the general public and elevating the collective worthiness of the human population.

Motive For Life

Motive For Life is a professional coaching, speaking, and publishing company dedicated to the personal elevation of self-worth throughout the world. The Motive For Life Program gets to the heart of the problem, the lifting of self-worth, whether it be with the individual or the organization. When you believe you are worthy of abundance, confidence naturally appears. You see opportunities that were previously

invisible. Confidence flows and motivation springs forth, from where there was none. Self-worth is the key to all advancement. High self-worth opens your eyes and enables you to accept the wealth the world has to offer.

A Motive For Life Coach is specifically trained to be your biggest fan until you are! Through a series of exercises and one-on-one coaching sessions, your Coach steps you through the program and guides you when the rewards arrive.

To contact Motive For Life, please visit our website:

www.MotiveForLife.com

CDM Retreat Center

The CRM Retreat Center is dedicated to extending the length of sobriety of persons seeking help from alcohol and drugs. We believe building strong recovery groups is the foundation of an individuals' long-term sobriety. Through our experience, we've found that retreats focused on the steps of recovery are critical to building strong groups. Strong groups are the foundation of an individual and the community of recovery.

CDMRC funds and promotes long-term recovery through strong groups. Our board of directors and advisory board have been running sober retreats for over thirty years. We have found that groups with an annual retreat are significantly stronger than groups without. We provide funding for men and women who are not able to afford a retreat but have the desire to attend. If your group sponsors a retreat and you seek funding of new members who cannot afford the fees, please contact us for further information.

To contact the CDM Retreat Center, please visit our website:

www.CDMRetreat.org

Printed in Great Britain
by Amazon